Dune Buggies

James Hale

MBI

Dedication

This book is dedicated to Kristine and Virginia

This edition first published in 2004 by MBI Publishing Company, Galtier Plaza, Suite 200, 380 Jackson Street, St. Paul, MN 55101-3885 USA

MBI titles are also available at discounts in bulk quantity for industrial or sales-promotional use. For details write to Special Sales Manager at Motorbooks International Wholesalers & Distributors, Galtier Plaza, Suite 200, 380 Jackson Street, St. Paul, MN 55101-3885 USA.

Library of Congress Cataloging-in-Publication Data

Hale, James, 1957-
    Dune Buggies/by James Hale
       p. c.m. -- (Enthusiast Color Series)
    Includes Index.
    ISBN 0-7603-1684-8 (pbk. : alk. paper)
       1. Dune buggies. I. Title. II. Series

TH 236.7.H34 2004
629.222—dc22   2003064586

On the front cover: The Meyers Manx – the fiberglass dune buggy design that started the whole buggy phenomenon may be nearly 40 years old, but it has now found a whole new following amongst car enthusiasts all over the world. Creator Bruce Meyers produced the buggy to epitomize fun and freedom. (Mike Key)

On the frontispiece: During the late 1960s and early 1970s, the dune buggy influence was everywhere. This is a glass Avon bottle containing men's aftershave lotion. The twist-off VW engine is the bottle stopper.

On the title page: This Fiber-Tech buggy is 'strictly street', with lowered suspension, polished drag-race wheels, full rollcage, eye-popping blue paintwork, and incredible attention to detail. (Keith Seume)

On the back cover: Wherever there's a beach, you'll find a dune buggy. This sparkling buggy looks right at home, and ready to play on these golden sands. (Mike Key)

About the Author

James Hale was born on England's South Coast in September 1957 and has lived in Brighton—the "city by the sea"—for the last 25 years. After graduating from art college, he developed a career in marketing and public relations, while also working as a freelance automotive writer and photographer. He has worked for VW Trends, Volksworld, VW Motoring, Total VW and Kit Car Magazine, and has also written technical books on modifying the VW Beetle and VW Bus suspension, brakes, and chassis for high performance. James is the world's leading authority on dune buggies, and this is his third book covering the worldwide buggy scene.

Edited by Heather Oakley
Designed by Mandy Iverson

Printed in the United States

Contents

Acknowledgments

Thanks to Mike Key, Robert Hallstrom, Mel Baker, Mel Hubbard, Pete Barr, Keith Seume, Henny Jore, Dan MacMillan, Auto Archive, and Mooneyes USA Incorporated.

Preface

Considering that fiberglass dune buggies have been around for 40 years, there has been remarkably little published about them. This is surprising, considering that they have had such a huge impact on the VW and Kit Car scene since the 1960s, and they are still incredibly popular today. I've tried to redress the imbalance by showing the buggy scene as it is now, plus provided some superb color photography of the development of dune buggies worldwide. The pictures illustrate the wide variety of buggies that have been made over the years and how their inventive owners have put together the same two basic ingredients: the chassis and running gear of a VW Beetle sedan and a fiberglass buggy kit. There's plenty of inspiration within this one small volume, even if it's not possible to cover every facet of the buggy scene.

Introduction

Dune buggies are all things to all men: surfboard haulers on the dunes, street roadsters impressing the folks in town, off-road competition contenders, and back-road bushwhackers on exploration trips. Built from fiberglass kits, they are the versatile, go-anywhere vehicles for those who want to create their own fun car, be their own automobile designer, and then do their own thing. Their kooky shape liberates

A worm's eye view of the Meyers Manx, showing the classic lines of the buggy designed by Bruce Meyers. His "form-through-function" approach to the styling has had many imitators, but the Manx kit has rarely been bettered in quality. The Manx has now made a big comeback, thanks to renewed interest in dune buggies generally, and the growth of buggy clubs worldwide.

This original Manx II buggy even carries Bruce Meyers' signature on the front hood. Cool paintwork, custom flames, and pinstriping make this unique buggy a multiple show-winner.

those who are looking for soul-freeing adventure, and their flamboyant colors and sparkling chrome scream "who needs a Pontiac or Corvette when I'm driving one of these?"

Americans are renowned for their love of the outdoors and for "doing it themselves," particularly when it comes to automobiles. So the development of the first commercially available home-build dune buggy kits in the 1960s was a sure-fire way for entrepreneurs to meet a previously unrecognized and untapped market. For their customers, what could be better than to have a rugged little fun car that could be built easily and cheaply and then driven across the sun-kissed dunes in California or across the golden beaches of Florida or the New England coast? The kit could be put together in a few weekends, and all that was needed was an old or crashed VW Beetle sedan to build from. A well-thrashed Beetle could be picked up from your local wrecking yard for just a few dollars, so it was inexpensive fun. Any kid could afford a buggy at a time when production sports cars were a dream beyond their reach, and everybody wanted one. Capturing the spirit of youth and freedom, they were fun roadsters that didn't just need to stick to the paved

Buggies have evolved from being a "poor man's sports car" to a niche fun car with a style all their own. This Surf Buggy has a cool interior, complemented by sports seats from a production car and a bank of aftermarket dashboard instrumentation. Speakers for the in-car sound system are fitted into a flip-up rear deck panel. Who says buggies can't be sophisticated? *Mike Key*

The beautiful fully chromed VW Beetle engine powering this buggy can be clearly seen when the flip-up body is lifted on gas rams. Besides the sparkling engine, the gearbox is also highly polished, and the underside of the body fitted with mirrored plates to make things gleam.

highway either—they were capable off-roaders and competition contenders, too. The dune buggy idea was to signal a revolution in motoring, creating a generation of car builders, leading to the development of a huge industry in aftermarket parts—both cosmetic and performance—for the buggy and VW scene.

From the very outset, Bruce Meyers was at the forefront of buggy design with his original Meyers Manx dune buggy. Mention the words "dune buggy" to any car aficionado, and he will almost certainly think of the Manx shape. Every buggy design around today owes its heritage in some way to the brilliance of Meyers' original and fundamentally simple design. The Manx was not the only design to help kickstart the buggy scene. Designs such as the Burro, the EMPI Sportster, and the Corvair-powered Road Runner were all there, too, but it was the Manx that provided the definitive buggy "look" that is today recognized all over the world. Meyers' design, working with the then relatively new material fiberglass, set a yardstick by which all others would be compared.

Despite the excellence of the Manx quality (some might say because of it), the buggy quickly to fell prey to copycats due to the simple nature of the molded fiberglass shape. With Manx production unable to keep up with demand, pirates soon found they could replicate the shape more quickly and more cheaply than the original, even if quality suffered. After a failed patent infringement lawsuit by Meyers, the floodgates opened to literally hundreds of poor quality kits and products by disreputable fly-by-night manufacturers. The industry got a bad name, and the

buggy image lost some of its sparkle. Meyers himself went out of business.

Whatever the problems, there was still a strong demand for buggies—they were winning races, showing up on TV shows and in films, and being driven by the rich and famous. If ever there was an unlikely hero in the automotive world, the buggy was certainly it. Detroit engineers marvelled at how practical they were, sports car owners claimed they out-handled the best from overseas, and wives and girlfriends wanted to be seen in them—so they didn't just have to be a second car. The diminutive size of a buggy meant you didn't so much get into it as strap it on. The steering was so light and responsive that it was like wearing close-fitting pants—you turned and the car turned with you. It darted rather than followed corners, it spun on a dime, and the pedal control was more akin to a Grand Prix racer. The dune buggy could outperform four-wheel drive vehicles, wouldn't get stuck in difficult

Like roll-over bars, wide wheels and tires are part of the traditional dune buggy look. Early buggies used widened VW wheels, but today there is no shortage of high-tech items to customize your buggy. These Weld aluminum racing wheels are lightweight and color-coded to enhance the overall look of this buggy. *Rob Hallstrom*

Performance of the humble flat-four VW air-cooled engine has been improved by the availability of high-quality aftermarket parts. Everything from counter-weighted stroker crankshafts, modified cylinder heads, performance camshafts, and large carburetors to Porsche-style fans and shrouds (as seen here) are available. The only limit is your wallet!

terrain, and could allow outback explorers to go deep into uncharted backcountry. As it had set out to be, the dune buggy was all things to all men.

The U.S. scene remained strong into the early 1970s when off-road competitors began to build increasingly specialized tube-framed "rail" buggies for racing. Like many fads before it, the American dune buggy scene took a dive as customer tastes changed, alternatives began to appear, and buggies were not so "cool" anymore. Even flamboyant metalflake paints were no

longer enough to create the sparkle to support falling sales. However, developments abroad kept the buggy spirit very much alive. During the last 30 years, the growing network of clubs has continued to bring buggistas (as those who own dune buggies are known) together to enjoy their cars, and media interest in these vehicles is once again growing.

It may be small, it may be noisy, and it may be cold when the sun doesn't shine, but dune buggies are so exhilaratingly fun to own and drive that these oddball

Enthusiasts often say they get more "smiles per hour" from driving their buggies than from anything else. With a big engine out back and plenty of wide rubber putting the power down, it's no wonder that buggy drivers have smiles as wide as a Cheshire cat as they cruise the highways. With off-road driving becoming more restricted, many of today's buggies are purely pavement prowlers. *Mike Key*

vehicles are still popular today. Times may have changed, but the buggy has remained true to its 40-year-old roots. But the quality of the performance gear that is available for buggies and VWs generally has improved since those early days. As is the case with similar classic designs, buggy shapes like the Manx and others have changed remarkably little. Why is it that we warm so readily to the buggy design and buggy ideal? Maybe we all want to fondly remember

a time gone by, to rekindle our youth, or just to enjoy our freedom. Or maybe the whole car scene is currently going retro with the new Volkswagen Beetle and new Mini and is crying out for designs that evoke a sense of individuality and style.

The buggy scene is now attracting a whole new generation of buggistas—those who might have missed out on the excitement the first time around and want to see what it was all about. Those who were there at the start are mainly still there—such is their enthusiasm for the whole period and the buggies they created.

Bruce Meyers himself has now launched an all-new Manxter 2+2 buggy to an eager and appreciative audience. His Manx club and clubs worldwide continue to enjoy the automotive self-expression that only the buggy delivers. Like those of us already hooked, one drive is enough to convince the casual observer that, more than ever before, the world needs a car that is just plain fun.

While the murals so often associated with dune buggies in the early days may seem a bit past their "sell-by" date now, there are still new buggies being built and decorated in this way. They may not be to everyone's taste, but when they complement a stunning paintwork and the sun is shining on a hot summer's day, who's going to complain?

Chapter 1

CREATION:

The Birth of the Buggy

In the United Kingdom, the most famous buggy name is the GP (standing for Grand Prix). The design was directly sired from an imported Meyers Manx bodyshell, though the wheelbase was shortened to allow the front fenders to give greater coverage of the tires. Rear fenders and the engine cover were also redesigned for legalization on the British roads. *Mike Key*

The Meyers Manx dune buggy was initially designed as a monocoque body/chassis unit to which the running gear of a VW Beetle was attached. It was later changed to a simple body unit that could be bolted to the shortened chassis of the Beetle to simplify production and to lower costs. The classic shape takes design cues from wartime VWs, cartoon cars, and early metal-bodied dune buggies. *Mel Hubbard*

It's easy to think of the beginnings of the dune buggy scene as being planted firmly in the youth movement and cultural revolution of the 1960s, but its roots actually go much further back.

The idea of a lightweight "buggy" had been around for a long while in the United States. In the 1920s, entrepreneurs began building light passenger vehicles to take sightseers for rides along the miles of coastal sands or right into the dunes—sometimes for fun and sometimes for profit. During the 1930s and early 1940s, dune buggies consisted mainly of stripped-down old Fords with the four-cylinder engine set well back to place weight toward the rear axle for added traction. By adding one or two rows of seats at the very rear, and with short wheelbases, big wheels and tires, and little bodywork, these early buggies looked more like agricultural machinery. The rakish and cut-down look of the buggy was nevertheless compensated for by outstanding maneuverability in the sand. Those who saw them on the dunes at Pismo Beach, California, and at Yuma, Arizona, fell in love with their performance and took away inspirations to create their own vehicles.

The WWII German scout car, the Kübelwagen, proved the strength of VW engineering during the war. The rear-mounted, air-cooled engine, torsion bar suspension, and excellent ground clearance were all factors that contributed to its military success in the desert. The same factors would eventually aid the development of the dune buggy.

Before World War II, there was another presence on the dunes—lightweight motorcycles. Kids had discovered the freedom of running light two-stroke engine motorcycles across the deserts, leaving behind the heavy Triumph, Harley, and Matchless bikes of yesteryear. The popularity of motorcycles among the young generation was so strong that competitive cross country and enduro events were being run in the southern California deserts. This love of the outdoors, and the realization that driving could mean more than blacktop and a white line, would stay with these youngsters when they returned from Uncle Sam's calling.

The devastation of World War II halted further buggy developments for a while, but a few good things did happen as a result of the hostilities. The first was that returning servicemen wanted to enjoy life after witnessing the horrors of war and also wanted to have freedom to travel the American outback with their cars. Suddenly there was a whole new meaning to going "off road." They also had a surplus of old decommissioned Jeeps, which had proved themselves so well during wartime. These slab-sided utility vehicles soon began to have their original flat-head four-cylinder engines junked in favor of something healthier. Besides the Jeeps, older cars that had

The design of the Kübelwagen was basic, but entirely functional. The Meyers Manx buggy followed this philosophy, being designed to allow form to follow function. The stand-up headlights, fold-flat windshield, and basic dashboard arrangement of the Kübelwagen were all design inspirations for Bruce Meyers as he created his off-road buggy.

been kept running during the war years were almost valueless when it came to buying new, so rather than trade them in, bodies were cut down, powerful V-8 engines were installed, and they became purposeful (if crude) dune buggies.

The second wartime development that provided a catalyst for dune buggy builders was the development of the Volkswagen Beetle. Brought into production shortly before the start of war, the Dr. Ferdinand Porsche–designed Beetle was introduced in Germany as the "strength-through-joy" car that was to ensure cheap transport for all in the new Nazi-led economy. The design of the Beetle was as unusual in its mechanical construction as it was in looks. With a rounded and

Another German VW wartime vehicle, the amphibious Schwimmwagen, inspired the Manx design. Its short wheelbase, high fenderline, and balloon-like tires would also heavily influence the styling of the fiberglass Manx buggy.

Before the appearance of the Manx design, other metal-bodied dune buggies had begun to be manufactured in the early 1960s. Among them was the EMPI Sportster. This could be built from a set of plans or be supplied as a complete bodyshell in two or four-seat design and be built around a VW Beetle chassis. *Mike Key*

aerodynamic bodyshell bolted to a platform chassis that utilized a central backbone for torsional rigidity, the car was both light and exceptionally strong. The chassis acted as a stressed member, and it was attached to the independently-sprung torsion bar front suspension, and the gearbox and swing-axle rear suspension, which were also sprung by torsion bars and trailing arm spring plates. Attached to the bell-housing end of the gearbox was the horizontally-opposed, four-cylinder, air-cooled engine.

With war imminent, the platform chassis and incredibly strong running gear was adapted to form the basis of the German version of the Jeep—the Kübelwagen (literally translated as "bucket car," due to its shape). Using main gearboxes fitted with outboard reduction gearboxes, the vehicles were endowed with superb ground clearance and tremendous pulling power at the rear wheels. The desert campaigns led by Field Marshal Rommel owed much of their success to the ability of the German troops to

This is Meyers Manx No. 4, named *Quatro*. Like the very first Manx, *Old Red* which was produced in 1964, it is a full monocoque structure, with no VW floorpan underpinning the design. The immediate success of the first 12 monocoque Manxes forced Meyers to redesign the buggie since everyone who saw them wanted an affordable copy. The Beetle-based buggie was cute, could go virtually anywhere, and could be built by anyone. Almost overnight, the buggy craze had started. *Mel Hubbard*

remain mobile in the soft sand using these vehicles. The traction provided by the rear drive and position of the air-cooled engine were key factor in the buggies' ability to keep moving in conditions where a camel would have struggled. The Kübelwagen, and its amphibious brother the Schwimmwagen developed tremendous reputations for agility and strength that did not go unnoticed after the war. Even their shape would lend much to the development of future dune buggies.

Back in the United States, among all the odd-looking machinery that was finding its way onto the dunes in the early 1960s, was a buggy built from a wrecked VW Beetle. These German cars had already begun to make their sales presence felt in America, and with their amazing tractive ability, it was predictably only a matter of time before someone would wed the VW

format to a go-anywhere Jeep-styled vehicle. The body had been removed, the chassis shortened to improve maneuverability, widened Chrysler rims added to the VW wheel centers, and flotation tires added. The buggy, built by Scott McKenzie, changed history. Besides the using the VW platform chassis, the buggy proved the adaptability of the Chevrolet Corvair six-cylinder air-cooled and rear-mounted engine onto the VW gearbox. The agility and performance of McKenzie's simple buggy in the dunes left other heavier machines standing, and its off-road potential was to be the inspiration for countless others. A wave of VW-based look-alike buggies followed, but yet many still looked unfinished, unsafe, and crude.

Joe Vittone made one of the earliest attempts to make a civilized-looking production dune buggy. He

Quatro is now owned by a French VW collector, but Bruce Meyers still owns *Old Red,* which has now been fully restored to its original specification. Meyers still attends shows in the California area with his successful Manx Dune Buggy Club and has recently launched an all-new long-wheelbase variant of the Manx called the Manxter. *Mel Hubbard*

produced a sheet-metal buggy built on a modified VW Beetle floorpan called the EMPI Sportster. EMPI (European Motor Products Inc.) had been formed in the 1950s to supply aftermarket parts and accessories, and as early as 1956 Vittone and his friend Les Prestwood had modified a Beetle that had been involved in a front-and-rear fender-bender. The damaged areas were cut away, and the resulting vehicle resembled a modern-day Baja Bug. The vehicle was continually modified with bigger engines, and the concept was developed into a kit-built buggy available for sale by 1963. Available as a two- or four-passenger model, the Sportster was constructed from 20-, 18- and 12-gauge steel and had a folding windshield. Kits were available in different stages and the company could even supply plans for those brave enough to fabricate their own angular metal bodyshell. Sales began slowly due to problems of obtaining parts from wrecked Beetles in the early 1960s, but it was a start.

Out in the dunes, one of the observers of those unfinished-looking early dune buggies was a gifted fiberglass boat builder, who just knew he could do better. Bruce Meyers was a talented artist, self-taught engineer and designer, and typical California beach bum who had grown up embracing the beach lifestyle. Meyers was a surf-lover, shaping boards and exploring Baja and the West Coast where he would surf, dive, and fish. To get across arduous terrain, Meyers used a VW Bus nicknamed *Little Red Riding Bus.* The excellent ground clearance, rear engine, and superb traction made him realize the versatility of the VW design when being used as an off-road vehicle. One day he was invited along to Pismo Beach to assemble and sail a new sand-sailer yacht. The design (not one of his own) broke up, but the day was far from wasted. While there, he saw some of the early crude dune buggies that were pounding the sands. They were big, noisy, and unrefined, but after a ride in one

High-Rise Baja Bugs

The Baja Bug came into existence as a way for off-road drivers to utilize more of the basic structure (and strength) of the VW Beetle sedan during long and arduous races. To help keep weight down, the fenders were changed for lightweight replacements that also allowed greater clearance for rugged off-road tires and increased wheel travel. The front hood and rear deck lid were also junked in favor of fiberglass items to save weight. The Baja sedan weighs about 1,800 pounds, whereas a bodied buggy will tip the scales at around 1,300 pounds. For competitions in the sand, a buggy is the only way to go, but on secondary roads or off-road trails, the Baja is a more comfortable alternative and has proved to be a serious off-road contender since the first Mexico Baja in 1967.

As dune buggies caught the imagination of the buying public, thousands of kits were produced. The growth of the VW aftermarket parts industry today owes much to the buggy boom of the 1960s. Metalflake finishes, chrome accessories, and flower-power interiors and hardtops were just some of the items available as the industry developed. *Mel Baker*

Meyers was hooked. All the way home he was designing buggies in his head, satirizing the buggies he'd seen with over-sized engines hanging onto them. He knew he would build one, maybe even sell a few, and they would be very different.

To get his ideas started, he first cut out the wheel wells of his VW Bus, fitted wide Buick wheel rims to the centers of the original VW wheels, and added 9.50x15 tires. The transformation was wild. Not only did the Bus look radically different (this was 1962!), but suddenly the vehicle could jump dunes and go into territory that was impassable before. Meyers could see what he would need to do to build his dune buggy:

use the rear-engine principle, add some wide wheels and flotation tires, and fit them to a lightweight, short-wheelbase vehicle. By doing so, he knew that he would end up with the perfect off-roader, whether he wanted to blast it across the beach or explore further into the outback than ever before. It needed style and form, he reasoned, rather than being a shapeless collection of mobile pipework with an engine and seats attached. Designs followed rough drawings, and he constructed a small-scale clay model to get the ideas into proportion. Meyers' wife Shirley even took on a night job to help get the project going—otherwise it might forever have remained a dream.

To give more power and torque to dune-driven buggies, the air-cooled and rear-mounted Chevrolet Corvair six-cylinder engine was soon adapted to the VW gearbox. With engines displacing up to 164 cubic inches, the Corvair provided terrific performance at a fraction of the cost of uprating the VW or similar Porsche powerplants. *Mel Baker*

The insatiable market for buggies provided some interesting sales opportunities for B. F. Meyers & Company. This Lifeguard Manx was one of a pair supplied to L. A. County lifeguards for use on Zuma Beach and was built on a new VW chassis back in 1970. *Mel Hubbard*

Inspired by repairing the chassis and the running gear on a beat-up Porsche 356 Coupe that he had bought, Meyers figured out the best way to build a unitary construction body/chassis for his abbreviated off-roader. Since the mechanical underpinnings of the Porsche were so similar to the VW Beetle running gear and engine, he took many of his design cues from the legendary German sports car. His one-stall garage in Newport Beach, California, became his workshop in 1963 as he began to shape his new buggy from scratch in wood and plaster. Having worked as a marine fabricator at Jensen Marine, Meyers had top-notch skills

The special Lifeguard Manxes had an enclosed rear deck to store rescue equipment, while surfboards could be carried on top. Lighting mounted on the roll bar gave extra visibility for night work. This example has been perfectly restored, complete with the correct decals and period fittings. *Mel Hubbard*

Since its inception, the Manx has been made under license in many countries around the world, including Australia, France, and (more recently) the United Kingdom. This English Manx proves the enduring appeal of the classic buggy shape. A blank canvas for those with imagination, the dune buggy is a customizer's dream, and no two buggies are built alike.

in fiberglass tooling and technology. He had certainly never forgotten the lessons learned in shaping components for cost-effective production: form must follow function and simplicity is the best design. Thinking of the vehicles he had seen at Pismo, including the angular VW-based off-roader of Roger Smith and Bill Chisholm called *Rivets*, and the VW-underpinned marine-grade plywood buggy of Ted Mangels called *Splinters*, Meyers married ideas together. He wanted the large wheels and tires that he had used on his bus to give flotation in the sand, the high fenders and short wheelbase of the VW Schwimmwagen, the stand-up headlights and simplicity of the VW Kubelwagen, and the totally open design of Italian "jolly" cars—all added together with a fine artistic sense of style.

The essence of the design was to be a stressed monocoque bodyshell that served both as body and chassis in one, with fenders around the top lip to keep spray from being thrown up. To replace the torsional stiffness of a metal car body, strong 2 inch mild steel tubes were built in to spread stress and load over a major portion of the panelling. This was similar to a conventional steel unit-body structure in automobile design. Inside the body, a tunnel was positioned in the central part of the driver/passenger well to locate the gearshift, as it would be in a VW Beetle. Cross panels and kick-ups added to the completeness of the monocoque structure to resist torsional movement. Attached to the steel bearers were the VW front suspension unit, the rear suspension, and the specially

Unlike many buggies that appeared on the scene, the EMPI Imp was an original design, designed primarily for road use. Besides the kit itself, EMPI specialized in supplying high-quality accessories such as Sprintstar wheels, aftermarket steering wheels, and engine performance equipment. *Mike Key*

machined aluminum castings that allowed the VW foot pedals, emergency brake, and other mechanical parts to be located. A Porsche-style hoop looped down from the steel tube carrier to pick up the standard VW engine mounts. This allowed the VW powerplant to nestle under the rear bodyshell lip for a professional, finished touch.

The resemblance between the buggy bodyshell and a small boat were plain to see, and Meyers used his knowledge of building fiberglass hulls to craft one that could withstand pounding from rough seas and big engines to good effect. Touchstones of Meyers' design included the 14-gallon molded-in rear fuel tank, the flat-topped front fenders (to allow a coffee cup to be placed on them without tipping over), an opening front hood with spare wheel, battery and tool storage beneath, a fold-flat windshield that rested on the front headlight bowls, a slanted rear bodyshell to allow a perfect flush-fit of stock VW Beetle taillights,

and the compound curved inner rear wheel arches, which were molded from the front hood of a friend's historic car.

Meyers' first buggy bodyshell was pulled from the molds in May 1964 and was christened *Old Red* due to its color and as an acknowledgment to the Kombi Bus that had helped inspire it. Once transformed into a fully rolling buggy, and with a patent taken out in February of that year to protect the design, *Old Red* was dubbed a Meyers Manx. The name conjured up a short, stubby rampant feline that had amazing agility and could move like a scalded cat. The emblem created to capture the spirit of the buggy was of a Manx cat holding a chipped sword aloft in a defiant gesture—a fitting image indeed. The buggy instantly became an attraction not only on the dunes it had been created to traverse, but on the road, too. Shirley Meyers, then an advertising assistant at *Road & Track* magazine, proudly showed the buggy to friends

The EMPI Imp was made road legal with the addition of a full engine cover and side panels. This ensured its success throughout the United States. Slick marketing, an excellent distribution network, and continual product development kept the company at the forefront of the buggy and VW parts industry. *Mike Key*

and colleagues in the Newport Beach area and immediately created a stir among others who wanted to own a duplicate of this cute fiberglass dune buggy.

Suddenly, and without the real resources to become an automotive manufacturer, Bruce Meyers found himself in business making dune buggy kits, still working from his modest garage. Working full time in the boat trade by day, and producing buggies all night to try to meet demand, Meyers soon ran into problems. His single mold was not enough to allow quick production. His insistence on producing only the best quality kits also meant that things were expensive. Even selling the kits at $985 (an expensive price in those days), he was losing money on each kit sold. There was the added complication that magazines such as *Hot Rod*, *Car and Driver*, and the newly-launched *Dune Buggies & Hot VWs* magazine had thrust the Manx into the spotlight on their front covers, adding further fuel to the demand for the cute little off-roader. Meyers was undecided about continuing with

the project, but took advice from his friends in the boat trade who told him to either raise the price or lower the production cost.

The only possible solution was to go into production full time in a regular production facility and to completely rethink the basic design to simplify production. Only 12 of the original monocoque-designed buggies were sold before the design had to change or Meyers would have been forever chasing his tail. His solution was again blindingly simple: rather than throw away the best part of the VW Beetle—the platform chassis—why not use it in a shortened form and simply bolt a fiberglass body to the top? After all, off-roaders such as McKenzie had been doing it for years before to great effect, so he knew it was a feasible concept. After cutting a platform to match to a modified body, things began to take shape. Meyers even sold his beloved Porsche 356 coupe that had inspired him to finance the building of the second pattern, the new mold, and the first body shell. In a stroke, the production problems

Produced originally for the Monkees film *Head*, the Manta Ray II Kyote buggy, designed by Hollywood car stylist Dean Jeffries, was quickly made available for sale to the public. The original design had sweeping curves front and back and built-in headlights. *Dan MacMillan*

of the buggy appeared to have been solved. The redesigned Manx could be made quicker, cheaper, and without loss of quality—the very hallmark of Meyer's design.

The new Manx looked similar in design to the original, but had a fixed front hood housing the stock VW gas tank beneath, a separate dashboard, and main body shell that bolted down to the VW chassis. The Manx Kit "A," as the kit became known, required builders to provide their own metalwork parts, lights, and windshield, but cost only $498. A more comprehensive kit at $635 included more of the parts needed for the buggy and was called a Manx Kit "B." The only complication for the buggy builder was in shortening

The short-wheelbase Kyote design was developed into an equally attractive long-wheelbase station wagon buggy design. Utilizing a "flat" VW Type 3 or Corvair engine, the buggy had a large internal carrying space once the rear seat was folded flat. Coupled with a two-part hardtop arrangement, opening doors, and tailgate, the buggy was the essence of practicality.

the VW chassis by 14 1/2 inches behind the front seat runners on the flat platform, but the job could easily be tackled by a competent welder. The resultant 80 inch wheelbase was fractionally longer than the earlier design, but nevertheless gave incredible ground clearance and maneuverability to the finished buggy and became the standard for nearly all U.S.–made short-wheelbase buggies for many years. The cheaper price and the kit's easy assembly turned the Manx into a wildfire success.

The long-wheelbase version of Dean Jeffries' buggy was called the Kyote II and achieved very creditable sales. It was also made in the United Kingdom and is still available to this day. The owner of this example has made a special rear seat and deck arrangement for a custom look. *Mike Key*

Here at last was a "serious" fun car. It could be built by businessmen as occupational therapy, college kids wishing to express themselves artistically, or seasoned off-roaders who wanted a more stylish set of wheels. Best of all, it could be licensed for the streets. This instantly increased the potential market ten-fold. Suddenly the newly established B. F. Meyers and Company factory was turning out three kits a day, then five, then 10, in a bid to match orders. The color-impregnated kits were available in tangerine red, royal blue, yuma yellow, dark green, or Corinthian white as standard, but were soon added to with a range of sparkling metalflake colors such as fuscia, emerald green, and brilliant red. Accessories such as flowered vinyl tops, carpet sets, special upswept exhausts, chromed Cragar mag-wheels, Gates off-road tires, and Manx-decaled gearshift knobs were all added to the ever-expanding Meyers' catalog.

The owner of this GP buggy has built the car with a retro look, including widened VW steel wheels, white-stripe tires, a vinyl interior and the classic EMPI logo on the front hood. Production of the classic GP design has been sporadic over recent years due to changes in ownership, but the buggy remains one of the best-known names throughout Europe. *Mike Key*

While orders continued to roll in, and the Manx became a media darling, Meyers' problems did not suddenly vanish. Despite his gift for superb designs, Meyers was no businessman. The continuing clamor for his kits by customers and magazines alike put him in the position of being in the right place at the right time but still without the capacity to meet the increased demand for his kits. No matter how fast factory expansion grew, and implemented new production techniques such as the use of fiberglass "chopper-guns," demand outstripped supply. Being a perfectionist, he wouldn't let a single kit out of the factory unless it was totally perfect, and the backorder delay rapidly spiraled out of control.

Sensing problems, unscrupulous dealers and knock-off manufacturers found they could easily

A capable off-roader, the GP was used in championship autocross events with great success, as well as being the "must-have" accessory for the fashion conscious in swinging London. *Mike Key*

Dune Buggies and Hot VWs was the first of several magazines to be launched in the United States because of the strength of the buggy scene. The first issue (far right) featured the Meyers Manx, and the buggy has appeared on many other covers since. *Auto Archive*

"splash" molds off an original Manx body and start production of their own to meet the demands of a hungry public. Manx quality was something that most customers wanted, but if it wasn't readily available, why not go to another supplier and get something similar, possibly for an even cheaper price? At one point, an estimated 50 manufacturers had copied the basic Manx design and were producing kits at prices that kicked away the foundations for the Manx market. Despite the protection of a patent, the B. F. Meyers & Company organization lost a landmark court case over design infringement at a critical time. The judge failed to recognize the basic fact that the Manx was an original fiberglass design and not one of the crude dune buggies that had been around for many years before. The loss of this test case allowed a flood of copycats to swoop on the rich pickings to be had in the buoyant buggy market. Meyers had also turned down offers from other big competitive

manufacturers who wished to become part of the Manx success and whose buggy sales Meyers had started to steal. As this possibly meant losing control of quality, Meyers' resultant "no" got others thinking that they could also develop their own designs and go it alone. This decision brought EMPI to the fore with its own fiberglass buggy, the EMPI Imp, to complement the metal-bodied Sportster.

Even with strong competitors entering the market, the Manx led the way for others, especially in racing competition. Proving its built-in quality, the Manx ran events such as the Tijuana to La Paz run in record time. A Manx also won the first NORRA (National Off-Road Racing Association) Mexican 1,000 off-road race on the long southern Mexican peninsula known as Baja California. In a field of 68 vehicles, a VW-powered Manx came in first, proving that this cute little buggy did what it was designed to do best—go off-road in style and go speedily, too. If off-road success wasn't enough, the Manx also achieved notable wins in both slalom and drag racing at events such as the First National Bug-In at Orange County International Raceway in California. The Meyers & Crown Manufacturing dragster *Purple Potato Chip* achieved a fastest time of 11.09 seconds, at 123 miles per hour, defeating the EMPI dragster in a best-of-three match race series. In the hands of Ted Trevor, the Manx also dominated U.S. West Coast slalom racing, particularly at the famous Pikes Peak Hill Climb where it won the under-3-liter class against a field of fire-breathing factory team race cars such as Shelby Cobras. Trevor's Corvair-powered Manx, and a similar buggy driven by Don Wilcox, ran in the under-305-ci sports car class, beating all but seven of the highly specialized championship hillclimb cars, including Ak Miller's undefeated 427 Cobra Kit Special. So successful were the buggy entrants that USAC rules eliminated the sports car class from 1967 to avoid ritual humiliation of "proper" sports cars.

The entrance of strong contenders such as the EMPI Imp into the buggy market was a signal that good quality, original designs other than straightforward copies of the Manx were possible and indeed desirable enough to keep customers interested in the whole scene. The Imp was designed to be a street car that could also be used off-road, rather than the other way around. With this in mind, the lines of the buggy were designed to be rounder, smoother, and more flowing than the stubby Manx. Seeing the problems that had befallen Meyers' company, EMPI wanted to ensure not only a quality product, but also that it was delivered to the customer in a slick, professional way through the company's extensive network of distributors around the country. To promote the buggy, superb brochures were produced, covering the vast array of different kits offered to customers. To ensure maximum sales potential, the Imp was also designed with side panels and an engine cover to keep it legal in all states.

Following in the footsteps of the Sportster, the Imp was designed for a VW chassis shortened by 12 inches (which provided more legroom for back seat passengers) yet did not affect ground clearance or traction. It also helped rid the buggy of the worst bump-steer characteristics usually associated with the very

Ephemera from B. F. Meyers & Company includes the superb "up the creek without a paddle" advertisement, and a fold-out brochure with Manx buggy kit and accessory details. The superb images on the right are from Manx Australia and were used in company advertising. *Auto Archive*

lightweight and diminutive length of earlier designs. The EMPI Imp was introduced in 1969 to universal acclaim. Customers purchasing the Imp were also encouraged to customize their buggies using equipment from the company's extensive accessory range, including Sprintstar wheels, sports seats, and competition steering wheels to provide the "complete" buggy package. With buggies becoming increasingly used in competition, EMPI also used the Imp buggy as a way of promoting the go-faster equipment from its range of engine and suspension parts. Like other forward-looking businesses, EMPI seized the chance to promote equipment other than just fiberglass kits. The company had realized early on that it would be this side of the operation that would become its long-term future if the buggy craze ever dried up.

With the promotion given to the U.S. buggy craze in the 1960s through magazines, it was only a matter of time before buggies found their way onto the big screen and onto TV. Producers rushed to get buggies into their shows and movies. After all, if kids loved these wacky fun cars, maybe they would watch TV shows featuring them. Maybe they would also buy

products advertised on screen with them. Consequently, buggies were used to promote everything from clothes and close shaves to surfwear and hardware. Sometimes the link was genuine, but most of it was simply marketing hype. TV shows such as *Groovy* (a pre-MTV music show), *Romp, Bewitched,* and *Cowboy in Africa* all benefited from having buggies featured in them. On the big screen, it would be movies such as *Winning* (with Paul Newman), *Live a Little, Love a Little* (with Elvis Presley), and *The Thomas Crown Affair* (with Steve McQueen) that would fire the public's imagination. Even the TV pop group The Monkees would have a special dune buggy called the Kyote designed for them by Hollywood car customizer Dean Jeffries and featured in their psychedelic movie *Head*. This would ultimately go on to become a uniquely styled production buggy in both short- and long-wheelbase forms. Again it proved that good design was possible without blatantly copying the traditional Manx shape.

As the hype of the buggy grew in the United States, it was not long before news of the phenomenon spread to other countries. The first sign of the buggy

The EMPI company produced some of the best brochures and advertising throughout the U.S. buggy boom. There were a multitude of different kit options available for the Imp buggy, and they were all illustrated in the catalog produced by EMPI, along with metalflake paint and accessory options. *Auto Archive*

Inevitably, many plastic model kits of dune buggies have been produced since the 1960s, and some are still being made today. This selection shows the Meyers Manx (boxed), Meyers Tow'd (boxed), Kyote II station wagon buggy (boxed), Barris "T" buggy (boxed), plus (in the foreground from left to right) a Sandmaster dune rail, two Bugle buggies, two EMPI Imps, a GP, an Albar buggy, and one of the many unbranded buggy kits. *Auto Archive*

Buggies have been used to advertise many different products, and to illustrate everything from magazines and books to LP record sleeves. On the right is a typical "period" sleeve for the Beach Boys record *Bug-In*, while on the left is the more recent Gorillaz cover. *Auto Archive*

influence in Europe appeared in Holland in 1966, where a Dutch VW-owners magazine ran a feature on the U.S. scene. It included pictures of the Manx, the EMPI Sportster, Roger Smith and Bill Chisholm's *Rivets* buggy, and Ted Mangels' *Splinters* buggy. The magazine had limited impact, though one wooden replica of the EMPI Sportster did get built. Just over a year later, the first true article on the Meyers Manx appeared in the Dutch car magazine *Auto Visie*. The feature showed the Manx in its true element on the beach, but despite excellent promotional photos and detailed technical specifications, interest was muted. Only famous Dutch photographer Paul Huf seemed to refer to this excellent piece while re-creating some of the pictures in 1971 for a cigarette commercial.

The European scene finally energized in 1968 when the German car magazine *Auto Motor und Sport* ran a major article on the U.S. buggy scene, featuring the recently introduced Deserter buggy of

East Coast slalom champion Alex Dearborn. Since the German language was widely understood, the story made a major impact, and European manufacturers immediately arrived on the U.S. East Coast to see how production could be started back home. Sadly, the Meyers Manx—the dune buggy that had started everything—was totally overlooked in favor of the more easily sourced East Coast buggy designs. In spring of 1969, the Autosalon motor show in Switzerland included a Deserter buggy, and later that same year another company called BAC (Buggy Autodynamisch Centrum) produced a close copy of the Dearborn Deserter. While other designs such as the Sandman buggy from Sandman Sales Inc. in Texas followed, none were Manxes. Journalists may have mentioned the remarkable likeness to what they called the original Bruce Meyers designed Manx kits, but—as was often to be the fate of the Manx—no one really seemed to care among all the hype.

During the buggy heyday, die-cast metal buggy toys were made in the dozens, with many accompanied by favorite cartoon characters. Donald Duck, Minnie Mouse, Bugs Bunny, and Snoopy all managed to get behind the steering wheel of their own buggy toys. *Auto Archive*

The Development of Sand Rail Buggies

As off-road race drivers and builders began to look at ways to reduce weight and improve the competitiveness of their vehicles, the solution was simple: forget using a fiberglass dune buggy bodyshell fitted to a shortened VW Beetle sedan chassis and build a tube-steel buggy from scratch. The lightweight, rear-mounted, and air-cooled VW Beetle engine and effective torsion sprung suspension could still be used, but were fitted into a custom-fabricated tube frame. The resulting sand rail type of dune buggy has become the favored construction for serious race competitors from the late 1960s onwards. Strong, lightweight, and still home-built, sand rails are the perfect answer for those who want to get to places the rest of the crowd canít go. Rail buggies are now increasingly sophisticated and have opened up a whole new market for family off-road fun.

But if mainland Europe had missed out on the fun, heritage, quality, and design of the Manx buggy, there was greater interest in it in the United Kingdom. As early as 1967, imported copies of *Dune Buggies* magazine had found their way into the hands of car enthusiast Warren Monks in Doncaster. The northern town may have seemed lightyears away from the sunny Californian dunes where the whole scene began, but inspired by what he saw, Monks built the first dune buggy in the United Kingdom from scratch and called it the Volksrod. Designed principally for off-road use, the Volksrod nevertheless took its basic styling from the Manx, even if it lacked the cuteness of the original. One year earlier, in 1966, a London-based firm of race car mechanics called GP Speedshop had also imported an original Meyers Manx bodyshell into Great Britain. This was reworked to comply with U.K. traffic laws regarding tire and engine coverage and was duly christened the GP Buggy. Launched in 1967 by partners Pierre du Plessis and John Jobber shortly after the Volksrod, the GP was far better placed in fashionable London to gain maximum media publicity. The first English dune buggy feature on GP ran in *Motor* in August 1968, and the dune buggy craze spread like wildfire, reaching its peak in 1970-71. The United Kingdom has remained a hotbed of buggy design and activity since those early days, spawning new designs and a multitude of manufacturers in the years since.

With dune buggies being produced in the thousands and the scene expanding so rapidly, many people began asking questions. The design of the cute little Manx off-roader may have started it all, but where would it end? Would the supply of used or wrecked VW Beetles that were so plentiful and cheap in the early days still be there for the buggy boom to continue? Would cheap copies finally undermine customer confidence in what was once a quality product? Things had grown so rapidly that perhaps even the manufacturers had lost touch with their original market.

Indeed, the buggy concept had grown so wide that a whole buggy merchandising sub-culture had evolved—everything from children's toys to LP covers were cashing in on the growing scene. Despite giving buggies prominence in the early days, magazines also started to get uncomfortable about covering the same basic formula each month and started to look at what else was happening in VW circles. Coverage began to focus on areas such as performance engine tuning, Formula Vee, and the burgeoning scene of competitive off-road racing. For long, arduous desert races in the United States, the original type of fiberglass-bodied buggies had become increasingly replaced by lighter, stronger, and more powerful tube-framed buggies. Focusing on this area seemed to be a logical development on the buggy theme at the time.

This was not the end of fiberglass dune buggies, but the scene was soon to evolve. The Meyers name was still going to be at the cutting edge of what was to come next, proving that the pirates weren't going to have things all their own way. A cheaper version of the Manx, called the Manx II, had been added to the range just a few scant years after the launch of the original in a bid to meet the copyists head on, and the Meyers Manx—the buggy that had started the off-road revolution—had notched up total sales of more than 6,000 kits. However, the next developments would take buggy designs to a new level.

Chapter 2

EVOLUTION:

The Buggy Grows Up

A dune buggy enjoying a day out in its "proper" beach environment. This is a Vulture buggy, looking every inch the archetypal Californian sand scorcher thanks to thoughtful detailing. The design was originally produced in the United Kingdom by Holmesdale Motor Traders of Kent. *Pete Barr*

Bruce Meyers' sophisticated street buggy–the Manx SR–was designed to meet the growing demand for buggies that were practical and could be used purely for pavement cruising. Produced originally in 1970, the SR design still looks ahead of its time today. *Mel Baker*

Realizing the problems with his initial Manx buggy design, Bruce Meyers decided to create a buggy that would meet two specific criteria: it would have to be lower in price than his traditional buggies and it would have to be lighter and more suitable for rugged off-road use. If he could do these things, he would have a vehicle that would appeal to a broader market of strictly off-road drivers *and* he would beat the problem of cut-price copycats.

Many of the Manx buggies were being driven on the roads to the outback, off-roaded during the day, then driven back home afterwards. Since the short-wheelbase Manx had big tires, low overall gearing, and a nonaerodynamic shape, this was a tiring exercise

for the driver. The buggy was great fun on the dunes, but it was no fun at all getting there and back. Also, the vehicle always had to compromise between being useable on the street and being set up for a hard day in the boonies. This led to a new line of thinking in designing an easy-to-build buggy comprising just the bare essentials. What could be better, reasoned Meyers, than a lightweight, tube-framed buggy that could be towed behind a Winnebago or station wagon, then unhooked for a day's play on the dunes? As a result the Tow'd buggy came into being.

If die-hard buggistas thought of the Manx as "too pretty and too nice" to be a good dune buggy, they found their salvation in the Tow'd. To make the new

Bruce Meyers designed the Tow'd buggy for off-road use. It had a low-price and lightweight design that utilized a tube frame as its basis, and minimal bodywork. By adding fenders, an engine cover, a front hood, and a windshield, the design could also be used on the road, and was christened the Tow'dster. *Mel Hubbard*

buggy both light and rugged, Meyers had gone back to the drawing board and thought through the parts of the Manx design that could be eliminated. Since the Manx was already a rugged, race-proven design that had set a new time record for travelling the Baja Peninsula, this wasn't so easy. However, in a flash of insight, Meyers threw out the heavy metal VW floorpan, replacing it with a strong, yet lightweight tubular frame that would incorporate the twin-hoop roll bars and steering column support. A vacuum-formed plastic cockpit liner would nestle into the frame, providing shaping for the seats together with a parcel tray at the

back. Fenders, the front hood, the windshield, and lights were all unnecessary for the buggy. Best of all, a retractable tow bar at the front was housed in the steering column support for additional strength and more aesthetic design.

At the front and back, stock VW Beetle suspensions, drivetrains, and engines were still utilized, but everything in between was Meyers' creation. The buggy was around 300 to 400 pounds lighter than most sports buggies, was far more durable, and was cheaper for customers. From Meyers' point of view, the tubular frame was almost impossible to copy without

Seen on the Manx Dune Buggy Club stand at one of the many VW shows throughout the year, this Tow'd is an eye-poppin' example of Bruce Meyers' second generation of dune buggies. Meyers himself raced a Tow'd in the second ever Baja 1000 race, but ended up crashing and breaking both legs. *Mel Baker*

specialist equipment, and the liner was formed on a press—something else that the average pirate would not have. Later models would have to be made from fiberglass, due to cracking problems with the thermo-formed liner, but this wasn't realized at the beginning. An optional front cowling was produced as a cosmetic extra, and this allowed the fitting of a windshield for those who preferred not to put up with the sandblasting received from the naked front tires.

The Tow'd sold well enough in its first year of production, but no sooner had Meyers produced a strictly off-road buggy than he had to reverse himself 180 degrees to come out with a street-legal version, too. The reason was very simple: although the argument went that the Tow'd was a trailer, in most states a motorized vehicle was not—by definition—a trailer. Thus, in order to be towed it had to be registered as a

car, which meant it needed fully road-legal road equipment such as fenders, an engine cover, wind-shield wipers, and lights. The Tow'd was also limiting itself to sales in the southwestern states where there happened to be plenty of available back country. In the East, there was more need for a road buggy. Buyers wanted the Tow'd legalized so they could drive it on the streets.

Meyers complied with an increasing customer demand and added some new panels to the existing shape to transform the Tow'd into a roadster. So it was only natural that he combined the two names and called it the Tow'dster. The new panels could be added to existing cars to create a very attractive dual-purpose buggy. A line of worthwhile accessories was also added to the Meyers line, including a cloth top and front and rear bumpers for a more finished overall

The Manx SR utilizes flip-up doors with concealed catches for a modern look and easy entry and exit from the buggy. Forward-tilting front hood gives superb access to the gas tank, brake fluid reservoir, wiper motor, and large storage area. The forward-raked targa top section accommodates a lift-off sunroof panel for proper weather protection.

look to the buggy. Despite the concept, the Tow'd and Tow'dster were always a compromise in the eyes of their designer. They performed well, certainly, but they had limited seating adjustments and rattled and squeaked more than the Manx buggy. Producing all the body panels in fiberglass also prevented the design from adding much to the overall profitability of the company.

On the other hand, the two buggies were a radical departure for the buggy industry that had grown up with the simple form-through-function design of the Manx. They were certainly heading onto the path that would be blazed by pure desert "rail" buggies in the near future, but Meyers wasn't entirely happy with

the concept. Sensing a movement toward more streetable fun cars, Meyers turned his sights back to the concept of the shortened VW chassis. All the basics were right, he believed, but he still needed a new body design. The result was Meyers' third master stroke of automotive design—the Manx SR (Street Roadster)—a sports car with all the functions of a dune buggy, but designed purely for the street.

Since the Achilles heel of the Manx had been the ease with which unscrupulous manufacturers had copied the basic two-piece buggy design, thus undermining the quality image of the Meyers company, Meyers was determined to make things hard to copy with the SR. The very name indicated that the Manx

The beautifully finished tan interior and dashboard of this Manx SR shows a remarkable resemblance to a production sports car. The collection of gauges ahead of the driver monitor speed, revs, fuel, and oil temperature, while the original 1970s 8-track tape player provides vintage cruise music. *Mel Baker*

Doing what it does best, the Manx SR (Street Roadster) heads out on the highway. This buggy, owned and fully restored by Dale Herseth in Arizona, was once owned by Malcolm Bricklin, who manufactured a similar fiberglass car with gullwing doors. Bruce Meyers even worked on the Bricklin project in the mid-1970s. *Mel Baker*

SR was the sophisticated cousin of the Manx buggy, designed for street or highway cruising. Launched in 1970 at the Specialty Equipment Manufacturers Association (SEMA) show, its aim was to fill the gap in the ever-growing street buggy market for a beautifully crafted and ageless design that could rival foreign sports cars, but was a fraction of the price.

In association with designer Stewart Reed, Meyers used all his skills as a fiberglass boat tooler to create a stunning new automotive design. The purely two-seater sports buggy had flip-up doors that made entry and exit easier than a conventional Manx buggy. It could take wide wheels and low-profile tires within the spacious wheel arches so that it was road-legal in all U.S. states. It also had a cavernous engine bay to accommodate larger powerplants such as Porsches and Corvairs, with the option of a power scoop on the rear deck to allow the installation of extra-large carburetors or air cleaners. It had luggage areas under the opening front hood and behind the seats. It even had weather protection in the form of the interesting, forward leaning Porsche-style rear targa top section to which a lift-off sunroof panel or soft top could be added.

Here indeed was an all-weather fun buggy that had production car practicalities, yet could be purchased as a kit for a base price of just $895. Made in 13 separate fiberglass sections (plus the roof), the buggy had a black grained vinyl-effect inner liner that was bonded to the two colored side body skins and to which the opening front hood, sliding rear trunk lid, and matte-black dashboard and cowl all affixed through the clever use of internal metal supporting frames and hardware. Even the two-part doors were bonded together to allow storage space inside them and to give a different inner/outer skin color like a real car. The design also required that no bolt heads, fasteners, or screws showed on the smooth outer lines of the sleek bodyshell.

Special vertically-lifting hinges for the doors were part of the hardware kit, which included all the rubber or aluminum extrusions that were designed and made especially for the buggies. The windshield frame was black anodized aluminum to compliment the rear targa top and required a specially made safety glass windshield. If nothing else, the design deterred the pirates, but its complexity meant that only around 500 or so kits and a couple of factory turn-key cars were

Modern Competition Rail Buggies

Buggies built purely for competition are a breed apart from those that see little use off the street. Here, what started life as a basic JSC four-seater fiberglass body ended up as a wild custom creation designed to tackle the boonies in style. Hallmarks of a serious off-roader include the wider than stock front beam, heavy-duty independent rear suspension, check straps for the rear control arms, nitrogen shock absorbers complete with reservoirs to harness the extended wheel travel, lightweight racing wheels, all-terrain tires, strong roll cage, and night driving lights. The bank of gauges in front of the driver enables him to keep an eye on the performance of the non-Beetle engine out back.

The Deserter GT buggy was developed specifically for racing by Alex Dearborn in Marblehead, Massachusetts. The buggy was legitimately developed from an earlier West Coast design called the Bounty Hunter. The Deserter GT was also produced in Germany when the manufacturer Autodynamics became involved in a race contract there.

ever made before the Meyers operation folded. Payments of back taxes to the IRS and the loss of business to the copycats caused cash-flow problems that ultimately led to its demise.

Despite the disappearance of the Meyers operation, other manufacturers were still active in the marketplace and were producing new designs. One such company was Dearborn Automobile Company, run by

vintage Mercedes restorer and skilled engineer Alex Dearborn, in Marblehead, Massachusetts. Initially drawn to the simplicity of Meyers' design, he was refused a distribution deal in the East, since this area was already covered by a VW dealer in the area. Undeterred, Dearborn developed his own buggy similar to the Manx, but it was based on a slightly longer 84 inch wheelbase to give better road manners, as the

The minimalist and purely functional interior on this Deserter GT owned by Christian Werner shows the race car heritage: a four-point rollcage, competition seats, and racing harnesses that complement the cool Porsche Riviera blue paintwork. The chassis is a custom-built unit utilizing just the VW Beetle central spine, which is fitted with a checker-plate floor.

The Mangosta buggy was a late entry to the U.S. buggy market, but aimed to appeal to those who wanted an easy-to-build design with more production car features. The kit was originally supplied with high-back, quilted effect seats, a choice of dashboard fascias, and a padded rollbar. Twin side-mounted fuel tanks allowed the design to have a low front hood and easier access to the fillers. *Mel Baker*

This Mangosta buggy, owned by Manx Buggy Club member Marlin Albert, was rebuilt a few years ago and sprayed in Corvette red. The design was a radical departure from the more traditional designs and bridged the gap between the declining buggy market and the VW-based kit car boom of the 1970s. This buggy was originally featured in *Hot VWs* magazine way back in 1969. *Mel Baker*

The U.K.–made Manta Ray was inspired by the Dean Jeffries-designed Manta-Ray II Kyote and was manufactured as a sleek one-piece bodyshell molding. This superb example called *Cherry Bomb* features chromed twin rear roll hoops, a rear-mounted fuel tank, and vibrant Candy Apple Red paintwork.

buggy would be street driven or raced. The engine and tire coverage was also improved to meet legislation in the eastern states, and thus the Deserter Series 1 buggy was launched. Later, Dearborn purchased the rights to a Californian buggy called the Bounty Hunter and modified it to the same length wheelbase, working on the principle that the Deserter buggies should be more sports car–like than purely suited for dune running. Thus the Deserter GT was born. With a sharply pointed front, curved windshield, and built-in headlights, the Deserter GT simply looked the part for racing. Better still was the fact that Dearborn worked right next door to the Autodynamics Group, which was one of the largest race car manufacturers in the United States. The group's knowledge in setting up car suspensions to outpace bigger engined race competitors was a key factor in the Deserter's development.

The Deserter immediately proved itself a serious race competitor in SCCA races at Lime Rock, Pikes Peak, and autocross events around the country. Since the Deserter GT looked more like a sports car, more and more sports car people started getting into buggies. Then, in 1970, Autodynamics acquired Dearborn's company, with Dearborn himself staying on to become marketing director and to oversee the development of another Deserter model, the GS. The "Grand Slalom" buggy was a radical departure from the norm, using a tubular space-frame chassis, designed to house a mid-mounted Corvair engine for optimum weight distribution. With a power-to-weight ratio better than any sports car, the buggy could hold its own against any Corvette or Cobra and had a top speed of more than 120 miles per hour. The Deserter was shipped in its various kit forms all over the world.

Many copies of the Manta Ray design have appeared in the United Kingdom, including the CTR and the Seaspray. This well-finished Seaspray buggy has the benefit of a monster 2.5-liter Type 4 VW engine with Porsche cooling fan setup. The buggy has run a fastest time of 13.67 seconds on the quarter-mile drag strip, but is right at home playing on the dunes, too!

If the Deserter was aimed at the racing car enthusiasts who jumped on the buggy bandwagon, then the Mangosta (Spanish for Mongoose), made by a company named Ventura in California, was a buggy for those who were looking for production car comforts. Designed by Karl Krumme, a Detroit car stylist, the Mangosta incorporated many ideas that were taken directly from large-scale automotive manufacturers. With a modernistic design as far removed from the traditional Manx-type buggy as it was possible to get, the Mangosta body was molded in several different sections, then jig-joined to produce a unitized bodyshell. Not only did this create a superbly rigid structure, but it aided assembly of the buggy onto the shortened VW platform chassis. Even the mounting holes for the headlights, the windshield, and rear lights were predrilled for ease of assembly. With excellent wheel, tire, and engine coverage, the buggy was fully road-legal in all states.

Besides the unusual body design, Krumme had also thought through the interior from a driver's point of view. Thus it had high-back, quilted-effect design seats for maximum comfort and even a choice of dashboard fascias in either walnut or padded vinyl. The Mangosta arrived late in the boom for buggies and production was therefore limited. Nevertheless, the few that do survive are a testament to a stylish and streetable design that helped pave the way for the new generation of VW-based kit cars that were to follow the buggy movement.

Dune Rails for Competition Sand Sports

Many of today's sand rail buggies are supplied as commercially available kits, designed purely for action in the dunes. Their popularity has soared over the last few years as more people want to drive these amazing, go-anywhere off-road machines. The basic frames come in a multitude of designs for two or four people, but often for competition use only or even for sand drag racing. The level of detailing on these buggies can be every bit as professional as on street buggies, since literally everything is on display for all to see. Sand rails come in just about every size, shape, color, and power from $500 "backyard specials" to $25,000 "experimental spacecraft." With the current trend in the dunes indicating more versatility, buggies are now being fitted with off-road race-style suspensions to allow them to do more than just go fast.

This Fiber-Tech buggy features single color, flawless sky-blue paint, and a full six-point roll cage for safety. This high-powered machine brings the whole buggy concept right up to date with its chromed full-dress engine and strictly street appearance. *Keith Seume*

On the other side of the pond, the U.K. buggy scene grew rapidly during the late 1960s and early 1970s. Many of the initial designs were inspired by the Bruce Meyers Manx buggy, such as the Volksrod and GP, but these soon diversified into a wide range of interesting and stylish buggy designs all their own. Among the more developed designs, the most memorable was the sleek Manta-Ray buggy produced by Power-on-Wheels, with a Kamm-tail and sweeping front not unlike the Dean Jeffries Kyote buggy from which it drew its design inspiration. The buggy even appeared on the front cover of issue number one of the most innovative of all British car magazines of the period, *Custom Car*. Proving its durability, the Manta-Ray remains in production to this day. The similarly-styled Seaspray buggy had built-in rectangular headlamps and a name that conjured up images of golden dunes leading down to sandy beaches swept by Pacific tides. Somehow, the illusion could never be matched in Britain, where the rainfall is greater than in California.

Another U.K. design was the aggressively styled Vulture buggy, developed by Holmesdale Motor Traders through extensive autocross racing. With its traditional buggy rugged cutaway look, one-piece bodyshell, and smooth front end with built-in head-lamps, the Vulture achieved almost iconic status in

the United Kingdom, even though the design remained in production for a very short time.

Since the boom period of those early days, the U.K. market has come full circle and is once more extremely active. Like the United States, a growing club scene has kept enthusiasts together, and new buggy designs are now being made by new manufacturers, thus allowing a second generation of buggistas to find their sense of individuality in an age of mass consumerism and look-alike cars. Certainly no two buggies are built exactly alike, and therein lies the attraction. They are cars that don't pretend to be anything else, unlike some other kit cars, yet they can beat "serious" four-wheel drive vehicles at their own game off road.

The first Manxes were portrayed as being able to traverse the most impassable terrain and frequently did. Other owners wanted their buggies to be sanitary show-quality hot rods or economy sports cars. The sheer versatility of the VW platform and a fiberglass buggy bodyshell allowed practically anything.

The dune buggy may never replace a '32 Ford in the affections of hot rod customizers in the United States, but for those seeking a low-cost, wind-in-the-hair fun car, the buggy is still hard to beat. Bruce Meyers, the founding father of the whole buggy movement, would raise his glass to that.

Chapter 3

BEAUTY PARADE:

The World's Most Beautiful Buggies

Jan Hermans' beautiful hot rod buggy was inspired by an American buggy seen in a German VW magazine. The color of the VW floorpan and suspension, engine case, seatbelts, headlights, carpet trimming, and even the speakers match the stunning metallic purple paint on the bodyshell. Note the details including the "peep" mirrors and the bullet-style front indicators mounted to the headlights.

Here's a beautiful buggy that is real eye candy. Joe Hogue's *Sweet Brandy* buggy has an "inches-deep" paint effect, with its multiple layers of Candy Brandy base paint and lacquer. The chrome-effect engine also goes as well as it looks it should, with many high-performance parts. The contemporary racing-style wheels and wide rear tires give the buggy a classic raked forward look. *Rob Hallstrom*

There is something unique about a buggy that makes it turn the heads of passers-by. From its cute and friendly "face" to its exposed wide wheels, tires and engine, and the rasp of its exhaust system, the buggy has a magnetism that attracts even the most casual observer. You simply can't drive a buggy and be a shy, retiring type, since onlookers continually want to ask about the car. They ask everything from the simple "What is it?" and "Did you build it yourself?" to the more technical "What modifications have you made to the VW chassis?" and "How much horsepower can you get from the engine?" The buggy is a genuine conversation-starter.

Some 40 years since the first buggies appeared on the dunes, they also are still creating a stir in automotive circles. From those earliest days with roots purely in off-roading, the once humble dune buggy has evolved from being an "ugly bug" and has been transformed into a "beautiful butterfly" by many of today's serious customizers. Interest in the buggy has grown steadily in recent years, with many of the current crop of buggies being built (or rebuilt) to standards that are more akin to show-winning classic car or hot rod entries at a concours d'elegance. Clearly, builders

and owners are lavishing more time, effort, and some serious bucks into making their vehicle the one that stands out from the crowd.

The current trend for building high quality "strictly street" buggies certainly isn't new. As far back as the late 1960s, buggies were being built purely for pavement cruising, and with the era of "flower-power" in full swing, it is hardly surprising that many were as outlandish and flamboyant as their owners could

The interior may be minimalist, but everything is exactly right for the traditional look on this buggy. The diamond-effect seat covers are a classic buggy style, while the carpeting is not fussy. The Scat shifter, rear-mounted polished fuel tank, sports steering wheel, and chromed roll bar all add a sparkle to this trick buggy. *Rob Hallstrom*

make them. Buggies were one of the first vehicles to seriously begin using the newly available iridescent metalflake finishes that had come onto the market at the time. Sparkling and vibrant, the glittering buggy bodyshells appealed to fashion-conscious youths. More interested in creating an eye-catching buggy, and without the desire to necessarily take it out for some back-country driving, their owners wanted their vehicles to snap necks, rather than just turn heads. Besides the shining effects of the metalflake finishes, buggies were also being equipped with a whole host of highly chromed, polished, or colored accessories that were being produced purely for this new and expanding market. Early buggy pioneers like EMPI were quick to take advantage of this marketing opportunity, producing chromed engine parts, exhaust systems, and

BUGGY FILE: Sweet Brandy

Builder/owner: Joe Hogue

Model: Manx-style (unknown manufacture)

Year: 1962 (VW)

Paint: Six base coats of Candy Brandy paint, plus 10 coats of lacquer

Front suspension: King and linkpin type, lowered 4 inches

Rear suspension: Modified 1968 lowered swing-axle type with Sway-A-Way axles

Engine: Bergmann 1,600 engine case, with Scat crankshaft and connecting rods; Engle 320–cam; Autocraft pushrods; Mahle graphite-coated pistons; Chirco 200-mm, 8-dowel flywheel; SLE polished and ported competition cylinder heads; Manley stainless valves with 44-mm intake and 37.5-mm exhaust; twin 45 DRLA Dellí Orto carbs; Scat HPC-coated manifolds; Bosch 009 distributor; STS exhaust system

Wheels and tires: 15-inch Weld Drag Stars with stock front tires and Mickey Thompson rears

Metalflake was popular on buggies in the 1960s and it is making a comeback today. Bill Newton's *Kentucky Buggy* has gold 'flake inlays blown over the emerald green 'flaked bodyshell, with some slick pinstriping to boot. The chrome detailing on the buggy is superb, right down to the eyebrow headlights and the air-horns on the front hood. *Mike Key*

BUGGY FILE: Kentucky Buggy

Builder/owner: Bill Newton

Model: Model: Rough Terrain style (unknown manufacture)

Year: 1969 (VW)

Paint: Green metalflake gelcoat finish with gold metalflake inlays and pinstriping

Front suspension: Adjustable ball-joint suspension

Rear suspension: Swing-axle suspension

Engine: Rebuilt 1,600 Type 1, twin 48 Dell Orto carbs, 40-mm intake and 35-mm exhaust valves, degreed crankshaft pulley, Bosch 009 distributor, Bugpack Mega-dual exhausts

Wheels and tires: Gold Striker wheels (14-inch front, 15-inch rear) with three-eared spinners fitted with Big O Big Foot tires 215/60/14 on front and 285/60/15 rear

The interior on Bill's buggy is another throwback to the early days of the buggy. A deep-buttoned green velour interior has been added, complete with gold edging to match the paintwork. Steering wheel is a 1970s-style wood-rimmed item. *Mike Key*

interior trim such as special seats, steering wheels, and shifters, as well as go-faster equipment to meet the growing demand.

Hippie fashion also directed some of the more unusual offerings on the buggy market in the early days. How about the flowered vinyl tops that were sold for the Meyers Manx buggy, or the paisley-designed seats that graced the interiors of many buggies of the day? As the buggy scene grew, so too, did the number of top car customizing shows on the United States West Coast embracing them, providing an added impetus for owners to buy the specialist parts to create their own dream vehicles. Even the earliest buggy-related off-road shows such as Bug-In quickly shifted from attracting vendors of purely off-road equipment to those supplying cosmetic goods for owners who were happy to spend money making their buggies look

good. This emphasis on aftermarket parts kickstarted the whole development of cosmetic and performance parts for Beetles that is still a huge industry today.

While some fashions have come and gone, the buggy has quickly adapted to newer trends that have emerged in the years since. Metalflake finishes has largely given way to the more refined metallic and candy paints of recent years, deep-buttoned dralon interiors of the 1970s have generally been replaced by quilt-effect vinyl seating, and gaudy murals painted on the front hood have been overtaken by subtle pin-striping or hot-rod inspired flames. Buggies are also being equipped with the best high-performance engine and suspension gear available on the VW and drag race market. These trends haven't simply been confined to the United States either, as the worldwide nature of the buggy scene has meant that influences

Adam Ferguson's left-hand drive candy red Renegade buggy is a U.S. design, but was manufactured and built in the United Kingdom. This sleek machine features a contrasting silver windshield frame and roll bar fitted with a high-level brake light. Wheels are lightweight CMS spun aluminum items imported from the States to complete the American heritage. *Mike Key*

A VW Type 3 "pancake" engine suits the low-slung back of the Renegade design, and it also has a matching red plexiglass cover fitted to shroud the fan belt. The rear lights have been sunk into the fiberglass bodyshell for a neat, finished look. The interior consists of black high-back seats, carpeting, and a sports steering wheel. Dashboard gauges are Heritage items with white faces. *Mike Key*

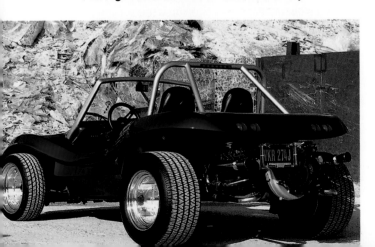

in one country have quickly spread across the globe. To illustrate the many ways owners create their ideal ride, here are five superb buggies that would be right at home in any automotive beauty pageant, yet are all very different in their style and approach.

Buggies tend to be infectious, and Joe Hogue's Manx-styled buggy is a direct result of seeing others out on the street. Having found an old buggy that was in need of tender loving care, Joe completely rebuilt the car to get it just the way he wanted, though only the fiberglass shell and VW chassis of the original car still remain—everything else was changed. Once smoothed-out, the bodyshell was treated to six base coats of Candy Brandy paint, and 10 coats of clear lacquer for a stunning "inches-deep" effect. The 1962 VW floorpan was sandblasted and painted before being re-assembled with virtually all new parts. This little buggy now features a modified swing-axle

BUGGY FILE: Candyman

Builder/owner: John Gurney/Adam Ferguson
Model: Renegade
Year: 1971 (VW)
Paint: Candy red, with silver screen frame and roll bar
Front suspension: Puma adjustable ball-joint front beam with disc brakes
Rear suspension: 1971 IRS (independent rear suspension) with drum brakes
Engine: 1,600 Type 3, stock twin Solex carbs, Ansa chrome exhausts, red plexiglass fan cover
Wheels and tires: CMS spun aluminum split rim race wheels (7x15-inch front, 11x15-inch rear) with Dunlop SP8000 205/45/15 in front and BF Goodrich Radial TA 305/50/15 in rear

transmission and a healthy "built" 1,600 engine that goes as well as it looks. The virtually all-chrome look of the engine is offset by red fittings that complement the luster of the paintwork.

Despite making a few mistakes along the way, and the fact that he had never worked on VWs before, Joe had no major problems with the project, which should prove an inspiration to anyone else thinking of taking on a buggy project. Going for a low street look, Joe kept the buggy minimalist, with an orderly interior and black carpet set. Quilted Jazz seats, a Grant steering wheel, a chromed rollover bar, and a polished alloy fuel tank are the main features of the otherwise fairly spartan interior. A Scat dragfast shifter takes the car through the gears, while the driver can check speed and engine performance with the Dakota Digital gauges set into the graphic-effect dashboard up front. The Weld Dragstar wheels and the ultra-wide Mickey Thompson rear tires are very much part of the car's overall look and along with a lowered front suspension give it an attractive raked forward stance. This show-stopping vehicle from America's heartland (Illinois) is very much the image of today's street buggy, with its clean lines, single-colorpaintwork, and chrome fittings and engine.

Buggy owner Bill Newton from Kentucky decided to keep his vehicle in a more retro style. This is a look that is fast gaining in popularity, as owners strive to create the period feel of dune buggies from the early days, but bring their mechanical underpinnings and performance right up to modern standards. The sparkling green long-wheelbase metalflake bodyshell on Bill's buggy has been left as it was when it first popped out from the mold, but has had gold 'flake panels added to the fenders and front hood and gold pinstriping carefully applied to finish the whole effect off. The green and gold theme has been carried right through the interior of the buggy, where the front Mustang seats and the custom rear seat have all been trimmed in a green crushed velour with gold trimming. The same material even covers the floor in a cool, checkered pattern.

Besides the themed colors, chrome is the main finish on Bill's ride. The whole engine looks like it fell into a chrome bath and can also kick out 125 horsepower when the accelerator is pressed to the floor. The brightwork continues with a fully chromed front suspension, bumpers and roll bar, headlights, fender mirrors, air horns, and VW turn signals. The horns were very much part of the 1970s scene and help complete

Metallic paints are one of the hot tickets on many modern buggies, and this Manx owned by Darren Razzell in the United Kingdom looks the part in its Peugeot blue finish. The RTTS graphic on the side shows this buggy took part in the "Run to the Sun" cruise in the United Kingdom—a special event for VW owners to support charity. *Pete Barr*

the retro feel. Not everything is old school, however, as the buggy has been brought right up to date with Gold Striker chrome wheels and wide Big Foot tires. A Grant steering wheel acts as the tiller and a genuine Hurst shifter helps move between the cogs. Up front, a bank of Stewart Warner gauges are set into the dashboard, including oil pressure and cylinder head temperature gauges and a tachometer and an ammeter. When the sun shines, this is a buggy that you can't fail to notice,

and Bill receives more than a fair share of attention as he cruises through the Bluegrass State.

In the, United Kingdom there have been more than a few show-winning buggies produced that are every bit as detailed as their U.S. counterparts. Englishman Adam Ferguson wanted to build the best Renegade buggy Great Britain had ever seen, and he certainly succeeded with his super trick candy red example.

The Corvette-styled Renegade buggy was originally designed in the United States by a company called Glassco of California, but was also made under license in the United Kingdom, where it is still made to this day. Adam enlisted the help of top mechanic John Gurney at Kingfisher Kustoms to create his dream buggy, and the pair started with an all-new bodyshell, a left-hand drive chassis with an adjustable Puma ball-joint front suspension, and an independent rear suspension. The plan was originally to create a 1970s-looking buggy, with a multicolored paint job,and slot wheels that were *de rigeur* at that time. Things developed into a thoroughly more modern machine, with flawless candy paint, recessed taillights, a contrasting silver roll bar (with high-level brake light) and windshield frame, and lightweight CMS spun-aluminum split-rim race wheels.

The interior is neat, without being over-fussy, using Corbeau seats fitted with three-point seatbelts, black carpeting, and a black Mountney steering wheel. Instruments include a 100-mile per hour speedo and fuel gauge and oil gauge from Heritage with white faces that are set off by the otherwise red fascia of the dashboard. At the front end, the Renegade buggy features a Type 3 VW "pancake" engine, which is fitted with a flat fan arrangement that perfectly complements the sweeping back of the bodyshell. The candy red and silver theme is carried through to some of the engine components, and the fan belt is shielded behind a red Plexiglas cover that also mounts the illuminated license plate frame. The Renegade buggy might have been produced originally back in the 1970s, but Adam's

This Manx buggy looks ready to cruise. The Type 1 Beetle engine is a 1,776 cc unit with dual Dell'Orto carbs and a Tri-mill stainless-steel header system imported from the United States. The Beetle rear light surrounds are painted the same color as the buggy, and the lenses are U.S.-spec units. The Manx kit was specifically designed to take these rear lights, and they perfectly match the contour of the rear part of the buggy bodyshell. *Pete Barr*

buggy certainly has no 1970s throwbacks—it's a tasteful and modern interpretation of a classic design.

Sometimes it's hard to better a classic American design icon like the Coke bottle or the Fender Stratocaster. In the stateside buggy world, it's the Meyers Manx that commands respect as the "definitive" buggy shape. So if it's originality you're after, why not build one of those?

That's precisely what U.K.-based VW custom builder Neil Griffith decided to do when he wanted a new project. He had always been a fan of the Meyers design, and when licensed production of the kits started in the United Kingdom, things were made a lot easier. The fiberglass bodyshell he chose was sprayed in a lustrous metallic Peugeot blue and attached to a fully reconditioned 1966 Beetle chassis, which had

BUGGY FILE: Sandblaster

Builder/owner: Neil Griffiths/Darren Razzell
Model: Meyers Manx
Year: 1966 (VW)
Paint: Peugeot 406 deep metallic blue
Front suspension: Puma adjustable, lowered 4 inch, with disc brakes
Rear suspension: Swing-axle, lowered and fitted with German Car Company disc brake kit
Engine: AS 41 crankcase, 1,776 Type 1, 69-mm Scat crank, Bugpack 4062-10 cam, Scat cam followers, 90.5 barrels & pistons, 044 CB Performance big-valve cylinder heads (40-mm intake and 36-mm exhaust valves), bolt-together rocker shafts, full-flow oil system, twin Dellí Orto DRLA 36 carbs, Tri-mill stainless steel racing-style exhaust, Pertronix electronic ignition, silicone Flame Thrower ignition leads uspension: Puma adjustable ball-joint front beam with disc brakes
Wheels and tires: Chrome modular wheels, 7x14 front and 8x15 rear with 185/60-R14 Road Champ Power Racer tires front and General XP2000 255/60R14 tires in rear.

The rear view of this buggy is all that most will see, as the 1,835 cc engine really packs a punch. Most of the engine tinware is chromed to contrast with the purple pearl paint. The interior boasts a TV set, as well as a pair of superbly comfortable Mod Plastia seats.

Once built, Neil used the buggy for a while before deciding to move on to another project, and the car passed to enthusiast Darren Razzell. Darren had been looking for a tidy Manx to provide the foundation for him to build on and create his own show-winning buggy. There may have been less to do with this buggy than most, but the engine was further improved with a U.S. Pertronix electronic ignition system, silicone Flame Thrower leads, and braided stainless-steel fuel lines. A set of stainless steel brake hoses were also added for performance and sheer good looks.

Inside, a Momo Corsa 12 inch leather steering wheel was fitted, along with Jamex solid billet alloy pedals, billet dashboard knobs, a Berg locking 9 inch short shifter, and a pair of four-point Luke racing harnesses. Ahead of the driver, VDO oil temperature, oil pressure, and voltmeter gauges were added to match the monster Autometer tachometer that resides above the dashboard. Even the needles of each dial were painted to match the tachometer, such is the level of detailing on this buggy.

In mainland Europe there is no shortage of well-engineered and beautiful buggies, and one of the best is the Hot Rod Sportscar buggy of Jan Hermans in Belgium. The original design of this buggy was, however, of U.S. origin, being called the Sandman and produced near Fort Worth, Texas before being manufactured on the continent.

Jan's buggy bodyshell was discovered as a wreck, having been involved in a car accident at some stage. Nevertheless, the potential was there to create a multiple show-winning buggy. Taking inspiration and some styling ideas from an American buggy featured in a

been modified with a rear disc brake kit to match the front discs. Motive power is courtesy of a well-detailed and healthy 1,776 cc Type I Beetle engine, fitted with Dell'Orto DRLA carbs atop 044 CB Performance big-valve cylinder heads and topped off with a racing-style Tri-mill exhaust pipe. Contrasting with the subtle hue of the blue paintwork are the chrome headlamps, modular wheels, roll bar, and a specially milled alloy plate that houses the Beetle speedometer and switches within the fiberglass fascia.

Jan Hermans' beautiful hot rod buggy was inspired by an American buggy seen in a German VW magazine. The color of the VW floorpan and suspension, engine case, seatbelts, headlights, carpet trimming, and even the speakers match the stunning metallic purple paint on the bodyshell. Note the details including the "peep" mirrors and the bullet-style front indicators mounted to the headlights.

German magazine, Jan set about to turn his 1972 Beetle into the buggy of his dreams. Once the body was repaired, it was sprayed in a specially mixed purple pearl paint. The color itself was chosen to replicate that seen on the U.S. buggy featured in the magazine Jan kept as his guide. Smooth side panels in the same subtle hue were also added below the body waistline, between the front and rear wheels. Before the body was fitted to the shortened VW chassis, the whole pan and underpinnings were sandblasted back to bare metal and then primed and painted in a contrasting purple paint. The front suspension was then lowered,to give it a typical buggy pavement-hungry look.

Engine-wise, the buggy has been increased in size from its original 1,300 cc to a healthy 1,835 cc by using larger barrels and pistons. The Type 1 Beetle engine has been beautifully detailed with chrome and matching paint, with carburetion provided by a pair of 36-millimeter Dell'Ortos sitting on top of polished and ported heads. Besides the eye-catching engine, one of the most interesting things about Jan's buggy is the interior: if you like entertainment, then this buggy can surely supply it! Up front in a special console is a miniature TV—perfect for catching up on your favourite shows while out cruising the dunes. Behind the occupants are the ghetto-blasting sound system speakers consisting of tweeters, mids, and woofers in a custom-built rear-seat housing.

The buggy has collected many trophies at the shows it has attended, and no wonder—it's a great little buggy that is eminently driveable, and is a class act in a world of other look-alikes.

BUGGY FILE: Sandman

Builder/owner: Jan Hermans

Model: Hot Rod Sportscar buggy

Year: 1972 (VW)

Paint: Special-mix purple pearl

Front suspension: Adjustable ball-joint suspension with drum brakes

Rear suspension: Lowered swing-axle suspension with drum brakes

Engine: 1,835 Type 1, polished and ported heads, 36-mm Dell Orto carbs, lightened flywheel, electronic ignition, Bosch 009 distributor, chrome buggy exhaust system

Wheels and tires: Chrome steel Mangels wheels in 7x15 front and 8x15 rear sizes, with Cooper 195/50R15 M&S tires in front and 225/70-R15 M&S tires in rear

Chapter 4

PUTTING ON THE STYLE:

Hot Paint & Cool Interiors

The Mooneyes dune buggy has to be one of the coolest buggies in the world. It's got the retro diamond vinyl upholstery, the metalflake paint, the chrome, the stance and, all importantly, the attention to detail. It is certainly one serious street buggy, but those surfboards hint that it can hit the dunes too. *Mooneyes USA Inc.*

Crank back the high soft top, stitched using one-off Mooneyes logo white fabric, and feast your eyes on the diamond-padded black vinyl upholstery. There are 1960s low-back bucket seats at the front, and there's more than enough room for a couple of bikini-clad girls in the back. _Mooneyes USA Inc._

In the VW world, just about everything that can be done to Beetles has been done: they have been raised, lowered, shortened, stretched, widened, and narrowed. Larger engines and water-cooled engines have been shoe-horned into the rear (and front). They have been raced, rallied, abused, and wrecked in the name of competition, and they have been loved, painted, polished, and chrome-plated in the name of restoration or customization.

Whatever their fate in life, the VW Beetle begins to reach a whole new audience when it is transformed into a dune buggy. Suddenly the metal-bodied sedan becomes a lightweight sports convertible, with engine, suspensions, wheels, tires, and interior fully on show and nothing hidden away from view. For the VW customizer who has run out of things to do to his Beetle, the buggy provides a whole new ballgame of automotive expression. Unlike a vintage Beetle that has to retain original body panels, specified paint colors, and exact period accessories, the buggy can be as radical as the owner wishes, with no two being built exactly alike. The buggy is pure art on wheels and doesn't pretend to be a copy of anything else on the road.

Producing a buggy that looks different from everyone else's, yet is eye-catching and tasteful enough to win the adulation of other owners, show judges, or simply those out on the streets, has become almost an art in itself. There is certainly no "right" way to build a dune buggy, and that is where the skill and enthusiasm of the buggy kit purchaser can be given free rein to create a unique vehicle. Paint colors, interiors, wheels and tires, and accessories can be as individual as the people who build them. And since the buggy appeals to a wide age range of enthusiasts—everyone from teenagers to those in their 70s—many different influences are evidenced in the construction and style of buggies. Hot rod flames from the 1950s and metalflake paints from the 1960s work as well on buggy kits as more modern graphics or subtle pearlescent paints of today.

The Moon buggy's interior boasts a yellow metalflake rubber steering wheel and gearshift knob (atop an EMPI shifter), not to mention the family of Moon gauges set into the unique wooden dash panels. Don't forget to wipe your feet on the Moon mats before entering. *Mooneyes USA Inc.*

Naturally, not all buggies are built for individual use, and many have appeared as promotional vehicles on TV shows, in music videos and as advertising vehicles for major corporations over the years. This is a trend that seems certain to continue, as buggies provide an inexpensive way to draw a crowd wherever they are seen. The following are some ways in which owners have used special paintwork and imaginative interiors to create a few of today's most stunning "show and go" buggies.

The Moon Equipment Company, now known as Mooneyes, will be a name familiar to anyone who has been around the world of street rodding and racing. The use of an unmistakable and dynamic Moon "Eyes" logo and famous trademark yellow color that was featured on Mooneyes race cars and hot rods throughout the 1960s has continued to this day. The company was the innovator of spun aluminum race-style wheel discs, fuel tanks, finned aluminum valve covers, and many interior products, as well as the

BUGGY FILE: Mooneyes Moon Buggy

Builder/owner: Mooneyes USA Inc.

Model: Dune Runner with "T-Bird" bubble front hood

Year: 1966 (VW)

Paint: House of Kolor gold/citrus metallic mix with gold metalflake added to lacquer; pin-striping and Wild West signwriting by Sugi-Saku

Front suspension: Narrowed, adjustable ball-joint suspension with dropped spindles

Rear suspension: Lowered swing-axle type

Engine: 1,776 Type 1, dual 44-mm Weber carbs, chromed Baja quiet pack exhaust system

Wheels and tires: Steel wheels with Moon discs, stock front with 135-15 tires, 8x15 in rear with F60-15 Goodyear tires

Driver and passenger are protected with a 10-point roll cage in this 2,332 cc-powered buggy, with wheelie bars out back to stop the front from lifting too far on hard acceleration. The one-off paint scheme was inspired by a similar design on a Kawasaki motorcycle. The green-and-blue theme has been carried right through the interior of the buggy. *Mel Baker*

The driver's view of the interior of the buggy shows the bank of Autometer gauges fitted into a custom-made aluminum dash panel. The light on the side of the "Monster Tach" lets you know when to shift gear courtesy of the SCAT shifter. Even before the nitrous is applied, the engine/transaxle combination gets around 200 plus horsepower down onto the tarmac when the pedal hits the metal. *Mel Baker*

Buggies are all about fun and style, so why not paint your fuel tank to look like an Energizer battery? Alongside it in the rear deck area sits the NOS kit bottle, plumbed in and ready to add the laughing gas to the air/fuel mixture when owner Michael Cruz wants to go racing. *Mel Baker*

BUGGY FILE: Cruz's Cruiser

Builder/owner: Michael Cruz

Model: Manx-type buggy

Year: Pre-1965 (VW)

Paint: Kawasaki motorcycle inspired green with blue flame graphics by Primo Custom, Reseda, Calif.

Front suspension: Fully chromed, lowered king and linkpin beam

Rear suspension: wing-axle with Transaxle Engineering gearbox and Super-Diff and Sway-A-Way axles; gear ratios are 3.78; 2.21; 1.65, and 1.14, with a 4.12:1 ring and pinion

Engine: 2332 Type 1, welded 84-mm DMS crankshaft, 94-mm Cima/Mahle barrels and pistons, modified VW connecting rods, Street Eliminator cylinder heads with 46-mm intake and 40-mm exhaust valves, dual Weber 48IDA carbs, Engle FK-8 camshaft with straight-cut gears, ceramic-coated Thunderbird merged header exhaust with Flowmaster muffler, Mallory magneto; full-flow oil system, 50-horsepower nitrous oxide kit; built by Rick Conemac and Russ Arao.

Wheels and tires: 8x15 Centerline wheels with Mickey Thompson 28-10.5x15 rear tires and 3.5x15 Centerline wheels with 135 tires in front

builder of cars such as the *Moonbeam* Devon sports car and famous *Mooneyes* dragster.

With well more than a dozen American rod, "kustom," and drag racing cars in the company's collection, Mooneyes decided to include a few VWs, including this special dune buggy. The basic buggy was a rather tired Dune Runner buggy when it entered the company workshops, but it has since been transformed. Using a whole host of parts selected from the company catalog, the Moon Buggy was stripped down and rebuilt using new pieces throughout. The low-slung body was removed from the shortened floorpan, repaired, then blown over with a gold/citrus mix metallic hue from House of Kolor. Then a large amount of gold metalflake was added to the lacquer, creating breathtaking results. Special automotive artist Sugi-Saku was responsible for the Wild West–style signwriting over the rear arches and the pinstriping on the body.

The interior is what makes this buggy special. Beneath the high soft top, created using one-off Mooneyes logo white fabric, is a beautiful diamond-padded black vinyl upholstery. The front seats are 1960s low-back style, and the interior also boasts a yellow metalflake steering wheel and gear knob (atop an EMPI trigger shifter), Moon gauges set into the unique wooden dash panels, and even Moon mats on the floor. If ever there was a great advertisement for your products, then this is surely it.

In the U.K., Neil Payne created what is undoubtedly one of the best Manx buggies around from the bones of a 1970 Bug. Built around a street custom look, the wild flame wheels and Hoosier tires add style to this pocket rocket. A buggy like this will guarantee you attention wherever you go, whether it's out on the streets, at your local shopping mall, or on the dunes. *Mike Key*

BUGGY FILE: Custom Manx

Builder/owner: Neil Payne

Model: Meyers Manx

Year: 1970 (VW)

Paint: Blue-to-red chameleon flip-flop paint with ghost flames

Front suspension: Adjustable ball-joint type with cross-drilled disc brakes

Rear suspension: Lowered swing-axle with a VSM Rancho gearbox with heavy-duty side-plates, welded synchros, heavy-duty shift forks, and a Super Diff

Engine: 1,600 Type 1, dual 40 IDF Weber carbs with a CSP breather box, Bosch 009 distributor with electronic ignition, 50-horsepower nitrous oxide kit to be fitted

Wheels and tires: Billet-style Weld Racing Flame wheels, 7x15 in front and 8x15 in rear with 195/55 Yokohama front tires and 245/60 Hoosier rear tires

backs before he got the shell looking the way he wanted it. Primo Custom in Reseda, California, handled the repair and respraying duties, and the zany paint job is a color creation inspired by Kawasaki motorcycles. The hot rod–inspired blue flames work well over the lime green, giving the buggy a fresh, modern feel. The paintwork is topped-off with several coats of lacquer for a rich, deep effect. With polished Centerline wheels and a fully chromed front suspension and bumper, this combination certainly sparkles in the California sunshine.

Interior-wise, the blue theme has been continued with the painted roll cage and blue center squabs to the Porsche 914 high-back seats. Ahead of the driver, a selection of Autometer gauges—including a Monster Tachometer—sit in the checker-plate aluminum dashboard. A Scat shifter is the only other interior adornment next to the driver, while at the back—where the rear seat would normally reside—are the nitrous oxide bottle for the injected engine and a cylindrical fuel tank sprayed in Energizer battery colors. This 1,300-pound vehicle shouldn't need kick-starting with any battery, as the 2.3-liter powerhouse out back provides plenty of horsepower to take on all comers on the straight quarter-mile, yet looks superbly polished and detailed for cruise nights.

Over in the United Kingdom the influence of the Meyers Manx buggy only recently took hold, with licensed production beginning just a few years ago. One enthusiast to fall for its undeniable charms was Neil Payne, a young VW fan who set out to build a very rod-inspired vehicle.

Hawaiian expatriate Michael Cruz might seem the perfect surfboard-hauling buggy owner, but his Manx-style buggy could not be further removed from the typical dune runner. A member of the Airspeed VW club in the L. A. area, Mike wanted a buggy that could cruise on the streets, yet hit the drag strip in style, and that 10-point roll cage and wheelie bars are a *must* on his 2,332 cc buggy.

The original body was purchased for just $75, but it took three months of hard work and a lot more green-

Off-road buggies don't have to be short on style. Rik Klaassen's Hot Rod Sportscar buggy is resplendent in its custom-designed camouflage paint, with olive green underpinnings. Monster tires, a Trekker front suspension, a VW Bus gearbox, and a Chevrolet Corvair flat-six air-cooled engine all combine to make this a supremely capable off-roader that is also street-legal. *Henny Jore*

Based on a shortened 1970 Beetle chassis, Neil's buggy started with a new Manx bodyshell, but before fitting it he took the opportunity to detail the underpinnings to the max. The axle tubes, spring plates, trailing arms, and front suspension were all treated to the same highly polished chrome finish. A Rancho heavy-duty gearbox from the United States was also added, providing the location for the well-detailed 1,600 cc engine fitted with Weber carbs. A nitrous kit was also rigged up to add 50 horsepower whenever needed.

The special effect of the blue-to-red chameleon flip-flop paint is what makes this buggy stand out from the crowd. As the light changes, the glowing color fades between a deep purple, then a sparkling orange, and plenty of other shades in between. With ghosted flame effects on the front hood, the result is little short of spectacular. Neil even has a crash helmet painted to match. Inside the buggy, the hot rod influence continues, with a pair of narrowed Recaro front seats that have been retrimmed in black vinyl with blue flames. The rear seat has been finished in a matching covering and effect and plays host to the nitrous bottle. The whole ensemble is an endorsement of refined and classy good taste.

Completing the rod theme are the billet-style Weld Racing Flame wheels, which are a definitive street custom look. These modern rims with their all-important Hoosier rear tires are very different from most buggy wheels, yet create just the right balance for this slick street buggy.

BUGGY FILE: Off-road Buggy

Builder/owner: Rik Klaassen
Model: Hot Rod Sportscar buggy
Year: 1963 (VW)
Paint: Camouflage
Front suspension: VW 181 Thing front beam and Beetle disc brakes
Rear suspension: Independent rear suspension with VW Type 2 gearbox, Porsche 914 rear disc brakes with Ford Scorpio calipers
Engine: 2,687 Chevrolet Corvair (six-cylinder) with Holley four-barrel carb
Wheels and tires: Mangels 6x15 in front and 8x15 in rear with B. F. Goodrich Mud Terrain tires

Not every owner wants to have a buggy that is painted and trimmed especially for shows. Dutchman Rik Klassen wanted his hot rod sportscar buggy to take on a military look and be powerful enough to compete seriously in off-road events. The camouflage paint scheme and Chevrolet Corvair flat-six engine were therefore no great surprise, yet a radical departure from today's buggy norm.

Basing his buggy on a 1963 Beetle floor plan, Rik didn't stop the modifications at just the chassis shortening. He added a VW 181 "Thing" front suspension to help lift the front of the chassis, then fitted an independent rear suspension at the back, and slotted a VW Bus gearbox into the pan to give the buggy strength and stump-pulling potential. Proving the adaptability of the VW/Porsche chassis components, Rik also added Porsche 914 rear rotors to help cope with braking duties of the Corvair engine. On straight-line acceleration, this rear-mounted, air-cooled engine, which saw original usage in a 1960s Chevrolet sedan and displaces 2,687 cc, will leave most VW buggies standing.

The Corvair engine is also painted to match the bodywork and runs a Holley four-barrel carb. The similarity in design of the Corvair engine to the VW's means it can be bolted into the Beetle gearbox using an adaptor plate, but the ring gear on the gearbox must be reversed, as the Chevy engine runs "the wrong way." Henny Jore

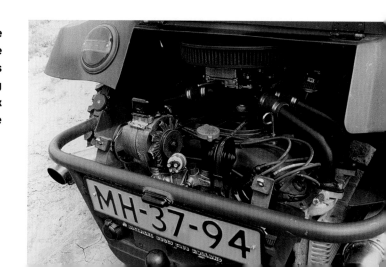

These are definitely the real thing! A trio of mouth-watering GT buggies finished in Coca-Cola colors look cool during a summer promotion for the soft drink company in the United Kingdom.

The paint scheme for the bodyshell was drawn out on paper before anything was applied to the actual body itself. The green, brown, and black scheme is carried right through to items such as the filler cap, fender mirrors, and even the central tunnel of the chassis. Even the engine shrouding is painted to match the olive drab color of the suspension, wheels, bumpers, and roll cage. The somewhat utilitarian interior has nothing more than a pair of wipe-clean vinyl high-back seats and full harnesses inside it. Overall, the look may be purely functional, but the car is anything but basic. Ahead of the driver, a bank of gauges is set into a drop-down access panel on the dashboard,

with some of the best wiring you could imagine on any car, let alone a home-constructed kit. Not only does this buggy work well, but its look inspired the rock band Gorillaz to include it on the front cover of the group's debut album. Now that's what you call style!

Promotion has never looked brighter than a trio of blazing dune buggies, especially when Coca-Cola puts its marketing muscle behind them.

The soft drink company commissioned three long-wheelbase GT buggies in their distinctive red livery to add the fizz to Coke's recent "Enjoy Summer" tour around the United Kingdom. The objective of the 20-date tour was to create a positive and lasting memory

Each GT Coca-Cola buggy was fitted with special twin cooler boxes in the rear seat area that held the bottles of cola in crushed ice to keep them at the correct temperature. The boxes could be quickly exchanged for fresh ones to keep thirsty customers happy on a hot summer's day during the promotional tour.

of the famous carbonated drink among younger drinkers by reminding them just how good it feels to drink an ice-cold Coke out of a trademark curvaceous bottle. The buggies were each kitted out with a pair of special cooler boxes that sat like Siamese twins in the rear of the buggy, holding crushed ice and glass bottles of the refreshing cola.

Coca-Cola graphics emblazoned across the sides, rear fenders, and the front hood of each buggy ensure instant recognition and, as if that wasn't enough, a special interior sound system reinforced the message.

This was all part of the sensory Coca-Cola experience, producing the familiar clink and crack of ice, bubbling fizz and cool drinking of soda. If you're feeling thirsty already, the idea certainly worked. With the sun shining and music cranked up, the Coca-Cola experience could be delivered in the way only a campaign of this scale could.

Whatever paint style or type of interior that turns you on, the buggy readily adapts to provide a blank canvas with which to create your dream. What you do with it is up to you.

BUGGY FILE: Coca-Cola Tour Buggies

Builder/owner: Kingfisher Kustoms/Coca-Cola Great Britain
Model: GT Buggy
Year: 1971 (VW)
Paint: Coca-Cola red, plus "Enjoy Summer" graphics
Front suspension: Ball-joint front suspension with stock drum brakes
Rear suspension: Swing-axle, slightly lowered, with stock drum brakes
Engine: 1,300 Type 1, twin-port heads, 31 Pict Solex carb, Bugpack twin buggy exhausts
Wheels and tires: Chrome modular wheels, 7x14 in front and 10x15 in rear with 195/60R14 Colway tires in front and 31x10.50-R15 Colway C-Trax tires in rear

Chapter 5

POWER SUPPLY:

Putting the Pedal to the Metal

John Leso's buggy is reputedly the world's fastest drag Manx and can run a 1/4-mile ET at 155 miles per hour. The short-wheelbase buggy is a crowd pleaser out on the track, but is a real handful to keep in a straight line when the power goes down. The ladder bars at the back replace the stock trailing arms and are there to prevent the buggy flipping right over as it launches hard off the start line. *Mel Baker*

Manx owner Rudi Mueller modified a 2.7 liter Corvair engine to produce a terrifying 200 horsepower, then shoe-horned it into his buggy with a KEP adaptor. With a CIS fuel-injection system, the buggy positively storms across the dunes. That nonoriginal rear wing is there to keep the back wheels down on the ground. *Mel Baker*

The VW Beetle and its derivatives have many unusual design features, not least of which is the engine. Indeed, the "flat four" air-cooled and rear-mounted engine bears more resemblance to a motorcycle or aircraft engine design than to that of a conventional car. The original design dates right back to 1936 and is generally credited to Karl Rabe and Xavier Reimspiess, working under the direction of Dr. Ferdinand Porsche, the Beetle's designer.

The engine design owes much to its location at the rear of the car. It was short to reduce overhang and light in weight to reduce handling and weight distribution problems. The first design displaced a mere 985 cc, but was subsequently enlarged to 1,131 cc and then 1,192 cc—better known as the "1200," which remained in production throughout the Beetle's long history. Developments to the design and capacity continued with the introduction of the 1,285 cc (1300),

Bob Yahn and Rudi Mueller show off their pair of Corvair-powered Manx buggies. Red and green may be complementary opposites, but these two dune buggies look right at home, side by side. The Corvair flat-six engines are air cooled with a horizontal fan powered by the engine's crankshaft pulley. This is perhaps not the prettiest of engine configurations, but they can produce between 140 and 200 horsepower. Sometimes function rules over form. *Mel Baker*

BUGGY FILE: Corvair Manx

Builder/owner: Rudi Mueller
Model: Meyers Manx
Year: 1972
Paint: Porsche Guards Red
Front suspension: Ball-joint
Rear suspension: Swing-axle, slightly lowered
Engine: Modified Chevrolet Corvair six-cylinder, 2.7 liters and 200 horsepower, fitted
    with Mercedes CIS fuel-injection system; KEP engine-to-transaxle adaptor plate
Wheels and tires: Polished slot mag wheels with Remington XT radial tires

1,493 cc (1500), and the 1,584 cc (1600), although the basic construction remained the same. As revolutionary as the VW's engineering was when it was first introduced, the unconventional design was the key to its success. The under-stressed, air-cooled engine ensured the owner with long life and reliability and also provided a perfect basis for tuning potential.

Dr. Porsche would hardly believe what owners have done to the basic engine since the first 24 horsepower prototypes were built. Modern derivatives of the "flat four" powerplant have achieved anything

between 200 and 500 horsepower and have powered racing VWs in many fields of competition—everything from endurance rallies and Formula Vee single-seat racing to off-road competitions and drag racing. Ever since the late 1960s and early 1970s, when the U.S. drag strips resounded to the thunder of high-revving muscle cars and Top Fuelers, the Beetle and Bug have been a force to be reckoned with on the quarter-mile.

Of course, today's specialist VW engines are radically modified versions of the humble VW original. The

BUGGY FILE: My Manx

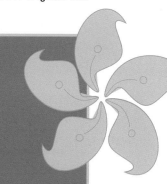

Builder/owner: Bob Yahn
Model: Meyers Manx
Year: 1962 (VW)/ buggy built in 1969
Paint: Emerald green metallic
Front suspension: King and linkpin fitted with Select-A-Drop lowering device
Rear suspension: Lowered swing-axle
Engine: Chevrolet Corvair 140-horsepower unit fully chromed, 390 cfm Holley carb on
    polished four-barrel manifolds, chrome buggy exhaust pipes, Crown engine to
    transaxle adaptor plate
Wheels and tires: ET IV polished alloy slot wheels with 205/60R15 front tires and BF
    Goodrich T/A 285/70R15 rear tires

Based around a custom-tube chassis, John's Manx is built purely for racing, without a fancy interior. Next to the driver's seat are the shifter, line-lock brake, and nitrous bottle. A CNC pedal assembly and master cylinder attach to braided steel brake lines to give plenty of stopping power. *Mel Baker*

availability of high-performance aftermarket parts for the VW and buggy owner has meant that it is now possible to buy crankcases off the shelf that allow capacity to be increased to more than 3 liters—a far cry from the original 1,131 cc of old. More than 200 different grinds of camshaft alone are available, as are race-style aftermarket cylinder heads such as those offered by Pauter Machine, Scat Enterprises, and others. There are now so many new components and performance parts available that it is possible to build a "Volkswagen" race engine which uses few (if any) parts from the Wolfsburg factory. For the serious racer this is all good news in the quest for speed and power.

Buggy owners have the added bonus that the engine is on full view at the tail end of the car, and many parts that are available also do much to improve the aesthetic visual appeal, as well as boost

performance. A pair of Weber or Dell'Orto carbs mounted on polished manifolds have almost become *de rigeur* for many buggy builders, providing reliable performance and sheer good looks. Other options include induction systems such as turbocharging or supercharging. Turbo systems are available from CB Performance in the United States, while the supercharger from Dick Landy Industries is an impressive setup aimed at both the street and off-road market and looks particularly good in a buggy.

Whatever you intend to use your dune buggy for, and whatever engine and hi-po parts you intend to fit in the business end, check out what others have done first before laying out the big bucks. To give you some ideas, here are a few superb examples of high-performance machines that leave others standing in the dust.

BUGGY FILE: Meyers Manx Drag Racer

Builder/owner: John Leso

Model: Meyers Manx

Year: Rebuilt in 1993 on a custom tube chassis

Paint: Metallic blue

Front suspension: King and linkpin, lowered

Rear suspension: Swing-axle, fitted with Porsche 356 brakes; ladder bars replace the stock trailing arms

Engine: Brazilian VW AS-21 engine case machined for an 82-mm stroked Bugpack 4340 crankshaft, Carrillo connecting rods, 94-mm barrels and Arias pistons with Dykes zero-gap ring,; Pauter machine camshaft, Melling oil pump, Super-Flo cylinder heads with Del West titanium 45-mm intake and 40-mm exhaust valves, 850 cfm Holley carb feeds a Tubonetics TO-4 turbocharger, Vertex magneto, 200-mm flywheel

Wheels and tires: Centerline wheels with drag slick tires in rear

When friends and fellow Manx buggy owners Rudi Mueller and Bob Yahn decided to add some punch to their vehicles, they opted for Chevy Covair power-plants rather than highly tuned performance VW engines. While the much-maligned Corvair was a flop for Chevrolet in the late 1960s due to safety problems, its rear-mounted, air-cooled, six-cylinder engine found a new home in many dune buggies of the period. Ted Trevor and Don Wilcox devastated the opposition at the 1966 Pikes Peak Hillclimb with Corvair Manxes, and Steve McQueen drove an awesome Corvair-powered custom Manx in the big-screen movie *The Thomas Crown Affair.*

The fact that the design of the Corvair engine was close to the VW's led buggy builders to experiment with adapting the unit to the VW gearbox. With the use of adaptor plates and reverse-rotation camshafts, or reversed differential units (the engine ran the "other way" from a VW), the unit could be bolted straight up and provided tremendous torque for off-road driven buggies. In standard form the Corvair turned out 80 horsepower from the 2,294 cc unit,

While the front end of the buggy uses stock brakes, the rear has a pair of Porsche 356 discs. Just in case, there's also a rear-mounted parachute to help slow the car down. Considering that the buggy is still using a VW factory engine case, John's quarter-mile runs are amazing. He's one of those guys with a "need for speed" and this lightweight buggy is the ultimate fix. *Mel Baker*

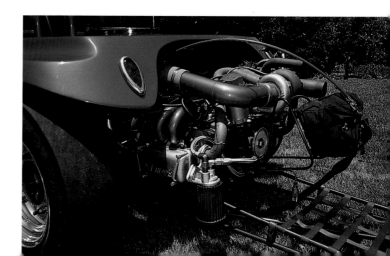

This is one hot dune buggy! Mark Philips wanted his Manx-type buggy to be fun to drive and have plenty of power. The buggy body is painted straight black, while the roll cage, front and rear bumpers, and side crash bars have a pink and blue paint–spattered effect. Based on a '69 Beetle chassis, the buggy has a Carters gearbox, Bilstein shocks, independent rear suspension, and disc brakes all around. *Mike Key*

quickly rising to 95 horsepower, then 110 horsepower and finishing with the 150 horsepower (2,687 cc) turbocharged version in the Corvair Spyder. And all this without expensive tuning.

Bob built his gleaming metallic emerald green Manx way back in 1969, complete with "flower-power"

interior décor and soft top. The buggy features a lot of chrome-work, but none more eye-catching than the fully chromed 140-horsepower Corvair engine, complete with polished four-barrel manifold and Holley carb. Rudi's 1972 Porsche Guards Red Manx takes the Corvair a step further by producing a terrifying 200

The engine was built by Roger Crawford at Heads Up in California and uses the best of everything. Auto Craft heads, a Scat crankshaft, Carrillo con rods, and a Holley carb combine to produce an engine with an 8.5:1 compression ratio that will blow your socks off when the loud pedal is depressed. A custom-built S&S header system blows away the spent gases from this killer engine. *Mike Key*

BUGGY FILE: Meyers Manx

Builder/owner: Mark Philips

Model: Meyers Manx

Year: 1969

Paint: Straight black with pink and blue paint spattered roll cage

Front suspension: Ball-joint, lowered and fitted with disc brakes

Rear suspension: IRS with stock drum brakes

Engine: Heavily modified Type 1 Beetle engine, with Scat crankshaft, Carrillo connecting rods, AutoCraft cylinder heads with 48-mm intake and 38-mm stainless-steel exhaust valves, 750 Holley dual-feed carb, turbocharger, and full NOS nitrous system, Hay's Stinger EIE ignition system, Mallory fuel pump, Berg oil pump, S&S header system

Wheels and tires: Polished Centerline wheels fitted with Toyo tires

horsepower from its 2.7 liters capacity by adding a unique CIS fuel injection system from a Mercedes. Way to go!

In California, the Sand Toy Capital, the dune buggy has undergone a tremendous renaissance recently as an inexpensive, fun car. Some of the older buggies and kits left around in the 1970s are now commanding high prices again and are being snapped up by enthusiasts who want to re-create the excitement of those halcyon days.

Not wanting to miss out, Mark Philips put together his Manx-style buggy on a modified VW floorpan, dropped in a full roll cage, then added one hot motor out back. The VW engine was put together by Roger Crawford at Heads Up in California and features the best of everything. The Type I case has a Scat crankshaft dropped into it and is fitted with race-style Carrillo connecting rods. Holding the barrels and pistons in place are a pair of Auto Craft cylinder heads featuring larger-than-stock intake and exhaust valves for perfect

air-fuel mixture combustion and spent gas removal. The compression ratio of this setup is 8.5:1.

Adding to the kick-in-the-pants feeling when the accelerator is depressed is a turbocharger, coupled with a nitrous oxide system for when Mark really wants to melt his tires to the pavement. A Holley twin-feed carb feeds the turbo, and ignition is provided by an electronic ignition system. The buggy is a perfect example of today's hot street buggies, where "go" is as important as "show." That roll bar might look cool with its paint-spattered effect, but it gives the passengers something to hold onto when this hot buggy goes cruising.

One buggy owner who has taken the concept of the "altered" drag strip vehicle and brought it right up to date is John Leso of Valley Center, California. Altered cars tend to use short wheelbases and light bodies, so the buggy was a natural choice when John was looking to adapt a VW-based vehicle to the format.

It's unusual to see women competing in drag racing, but Ali Southcombe and her race-prepared LWB GP buggy have taken on all competitors in the U.K. VW Drag Racing Championships and won. The car has run a best elapsed time of 11.35 seconds at 116.78 miles per hour using a Type 1 Beetle engine and still running on a stock VW chassis. A Hurst line-lock holds the front of the buggy still while "burning out" the rear tires. *Mike Key*

His Meyers Manx racer still uses a VW factory case as the basis for the powerplant, yet he's already hit a 9.01 elapsed time at a speed of 155 miles per hour. The Brazilian AS21 engine case has had the magic of Jason Lauffer of VW Paradise in San Marcos, California, worked on it, though. An 82-millimeter stroke, forged 4340 Bugpack crankshaft has been fitted within the machined case, and 94-millimeter barrels

and pistons were added to give a total displacement of 2,276 cc. Carrillo rods connect the crank to the Arias pistons, and the compression ratio of the whole setup has been kept to a modest 8.25:1.

John decided that the shortened VW floorpan wasn't quite strong enough or light enough for his purposes, so he had an all-new tube chassis built out of chromoly tubing to handle the power. The buggy

BUGGY FILE: El Diablo

Builder/owner: Ali & Dave Southcombe
Model: GP Super Buggy
Year: 1960 (VW)
Paint: Purple pearl
Front suspension: King and Linkpin lowered with Sway-A-Way adjusters
Rear suspension: Swing-axle, lowered
Engine: 2,332 Type 1, Bugpack wedge-mated 84-mm stroke crankshaft, 94-mm Mahle barrels and pistons, Bugpack race connecting rods, Engle FK89 camshaft, reworked Super Flow II cylinder heads with 44-mm inlet and 37-mm exhaust valves, Berg 1.45:1 ratio rockers, Berg full-flow 30-mm oil pump, twin Weber 48IDA carbs, MSD ignition module, merged exhaust system
Wheels and tires: Erco 3.5x15 aluminum wheels in front with Continental 135/70x15 tires, Douglas 7x15 spun aluminum wheels in rear with 26x8.5 Mickey Thompson slicks

still runs on a lowered linkpin front axle and a swing-axle VW rear suspension, but it is fitted with Porsche 356 rear brakes, just in case. A parachute attached to the back of the car is John's insurance policy that he'll stop at the far end of the quarter-mile track. Ladder bars at the rear also provide peace of mind when John launches the buggy hard and help get the front wheels back down on the ground. At a weight of just 1,409 pounds, including John, the Manx is a fly-weight that can start getting very hard to hold in a straight line at any speed, let alone more than 100 miles per hour.

Everything about this buggy shows it is built for speed, and it is a great crowd pleaser at events on the track. Just watch for the blue blur as it scorches the tarmac at a raceway near you.

In the United Kingdom it's the young women who are some of the quickest buggy drivers out on the drag strip. Ali Southcombe had been hooked on speed for a long time before she met her future partner, Dave, who

The business end of the GP buggy shows off the 2,332 cc Type I engine, complete with 48 IDA Webers and modified Super Flow cylinder heads. Two fans provide the cooling air over the barrels and heads, while a Berg full-flow oil system helps keep the engine lubricant cool and moving. The buggy is regularly entered in PRO ET classes alongside professional V-8 race teams, as well as in the VW classes. *Mike Key*

The Simpson parachute and Gene Berg wheelie bars are a must on this super-quick dragster buggy. A CNC staging brake helps hold the buggy on the starting line but, once released, all you'll see is a yellow blur as the buggy launches down the drag strip. *Henny Jore*

modified Super Flo cylinder heads. This combination has already taken Ali and the buggy to a best time of 11.35 seconds at 116.78 miles per hour. As a bonus, since the buggy is stock Beetle length, straight-line stability is better than most.

The buggy certainly looks a million dollars in its professionally sprayed El Diablo purple and airbrushed signwriting. Inside there are few creature comforts or luxuries such as carpets or speedometers—this is a full-on race car, after all! Everything unnecessary has been removed to save weight, though all the parts remaining have been fully rebuilt for safety. One addition was a Hurst line lock to hold the front still while burning out.

Consistent placements in strong fields of drag racers have proved that young women like Ali are every bit as good as the guys when it comes to going fast. Certainly this is one buggy that is truly smokin'.

Building high-powered drag race buggies is not just a phenomenon that is confined to the United States. In Europe, builders have been putting together superb machinery for many years, and the eye-poppin' canary yellow Hot Rod Sportscar buggy of Pieter Mooijman in the Netherlands is one of the best.

The basis of Pieter's buggy is a shortened 1967 Beetle chassis, but it is equipped with independent rear suspension to provide better handling. The cockpit of the buggy is completely stripped-out, with just a driver's seat inside plus, not unnaturally, a full roll cage, just in case this buggy gets "on its head." Mounted on the rear deck is the Simpson parachute— a necessary feature to try to slow this flyweight buggy

introduced her to the world of VW drag racing. Her 1970s-style GP long-wheelbase buggy was soon transformed into a very respectable racer, where Ali scored an 18.13 elapsed time over the standing quarter-mile on its first outing. The buggy started racing with a Type 4 engine, but this was soon exchanged for a killer Type 1 engine, with a 2,332 cc displacement.

Built around a factory case, the Beetle engine has been fitted with a Bugpack wedgemated 84-millimeter stroke crankshaft and 94-millimeter Mahle barrels and pistons. Bugpack race rods with ARP2000 bolts were used to connect them, while the favorite drag racing Engle FK89 camshaft operates the valves in the

BUGGY FILE: Dragster Buggy

Builder/owner: Pieter Mooijman

Model: Hot Rod Sportscar

Year: 1967 (VW)

Paint: Canary yellow

Front suspension: Ball-joint with disc brakes

Rear suspension: IRS with drum brakes

Engine: 2,369 Type 2 Bus engine with Porsche-style upright fan conversion, turbocharger with NOS nitrous oxide system, EFI fuel-injection system, custom header system

Wheels and tires: Centerline 3.5x15 with Michelin XZX 135x15 tires in front and Convo 8.5x15 with Goodyear Eagle 26x15 slick tires in rear.

down at the end of the quarter-mile. Powering it up the strip is a Type 2 VW Bus engine, modified with a Porsche-style upright fan conversion—a common modification in Europe. The engine has a capacity of 2,369 cc, aided by a turbocharging system, an EFI fuel injection system, and a full nitrous oxide kit to apply the extra gas when needed.

Since the buggy can easily pull wheelies as it launches away from the start line, Gene Berg ladder bars are fitted at the rear to stop it from flipping over when the front wheels lift off the tarmac. A CNC staging brake holds the buggy until the green light shows.

This is one hot buggy you can't miss out on the drag strip.

The pro-built drag racing Hot Rod Sportscar buggy of Pieter Mooijman in Holland is a master-piece of VW engineering. The 1,320-pound.buggy uses a 2,369 cc Type 2 engine fitted with a turbo and nitrous system and has a com-pression ratio of 8.5:1. An Autometer Monster Tach with shift lights dominates the driver's view and is mounted to the front hood. *Henny Jore*

Chapter 6

CLUBBING TOGETHER:

Enjoying the Buggy Scene

In mainland Europe, VW Euro is regarded as the premier annual event, attracting visitors from around the world. There is always a large buggy contingent present, and owners are keen to compete in the off-road events organized during the show. Short-course races over hills and through gullies against the clock remain a favorite, though a drag-race through mud isn't far behind.

A buggy exhibits its off-road potential at a short-course off-road event. Spectator events like these are hugely popular among the buggy club scene throughout the world.

Volkswagen enthusiasts tend to be some of the friendliest folk on the planet. Owning a Beetle or Bus is like having a membership in an exclusive club throughout the world—everywhere you go you will be welcomed with a camaraderie that is unique in automotive circles.

Building or owning a dune buggy seems to take that membership a step beyond. Since there are fewer buggies around than the Beetles from which they were originally built, it is inevitable that the buggy community is smaller and consequently tighter-knit than for other types of VW-related vehicles. Like other vehicle owners, buggistas also tend to set up their own clubs—sometimes just as a social gathering or a way to meet up with other like-minded enthusiasts at the larger VW events. Buggy clubs, and organizations promoting events involving buggies, have been around since the dawn of the buggy movement itself. Some even existed before the advent of the first

fiberglass-bodied buggies. Clubs are a great way to find out what's hot news on the buggy scene, swap stories, trade parts, or help others out with advice on their buggy building.

Like their vehicles, buggistas tend to fall into certain types, depending what area of the dune buggy scene they are interested in. The most obvious area is off-road and competitive events. The real forte of the buggy has always been in its ability to traverse difficult terrain, and it became a natural in competitive events that previously had been dominated by motorcyclists and jeep owners. Right from the first flurry of buggy-building activity in the 1960s, buggy owners began to get involved in low-key and low-budget racing events in the dunes as a first step into more competitive events.

Buggy owners and builders who are preparing their buggies for racing are serious about the construction of their vehicles and strive to have the

The Manx Dune Buggy Club regularly has a presence at large VW shows and always turns up many interesting and historic vehicles. As the sticker on this buggy states: "This oldest Meyers Manx is also Baja's first record breaker. Driven nonstop with 65 gallons of gas. The four-year-old bike record was beaten by over five hours, culminating in the formation of Mexican 1000, 1967." This was the very buggy driven by Bruce Meyers and Ted Mangels to create the record of 34 hours and 45 minutes on the Baja peninsula between La Paz and Tijuana. *Mel Baker*

strongest, lightest, and most durable parts for their buggies. They know that everything about the buggy will have to stand up to the rigors of harsh usage over rocky backcountry trails and inhospitable deserts. Mechanical failures miles from anywhere are not an option. Even with short-course racing or friendly club runs into the mountains, careful preparation for off-road racing is essential. These guys live and breathe transaxles, air filters, skid plates, beefed-up suspensions, and roll cages.

The ultimate challenge for buggies is during races such as the Baja 1000, near the Mexican border in California, where men and machines are tested to the limit. These are serious racing events, more suitable now for factory-sponsored teams, but this is the very event that was dominated by the Meyers Manx in the 1960s and some fiberglass buggies still compete to this day. While such events are the ultimate test for a racing buggy, there are plenty of other off-road style events that are not so rigorous, but are still great fun

Club events are a great place to meet other owners and to check out their cars. If you're thinking of buying a buggy, then club meetings like these also provide an excellent opportunity to talk to buggy builders and assess what is required to build a buggy. While you will have to buy the buggy kit, the advice usually comes free. This cute buggy is a Signature Series Manx. *Mel Baker*

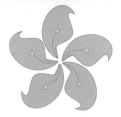

This ultraclean drag race buggy was on display at VW Classic, one of the largest VW shows in California. Traders usually offer special prices on their wares at shows, so take advantage of the opportunity to collect the parts for your buggy without paying top-dollar prices. *Mel Baker*

for owners to use their buggies in. VW shows and buggy club events usually have an off-road course prepared for those who want to try some mud-plugging and hill climbing. A favorite spectator sport is watching buggies compete on the short off-road course at large VW events such as VW Euro in Europe and similar events in the United States. Courses are designed to eliminate the unwary with water gullies, steep banks, and slippery hills to traverse, and all against the clock.

Other clubs cater not only to the boonie-bashers, but to those owners of fiberglass-bodied street buggies that see occasional use off the road. The Manx Dune Buggy Club, for example, organizes events to please these owners, too. Here, the buggistas like to participate with less-strenuous fun driving events. Regular cruises are organized through the beautiful scenery of the American outback or become camping outings in Nevada, but do not run over terrain that is seriously going to challenge the mechanical construction of the buggies. It's a great, relaxed atmosphere for everyone to eyeball their club members' cars, talk about the good times of buggy ownership, and down a few beers around the campfire.

With street buggies, the emphasis is more on having a respectable buggy that is well-constructed rather than a "built-to-the-max" competitive racer. The club community is a real asset here, as parts can usually be bought and sold at club meetings without the need for top-dollar prices. For the price of a small membership

The Manx Club organizes a variety of different events throughout the year to get buggy owners together and to have real fun. Besides the static gatherings at VW events, the club organizes desert runs, camping trips into the outback, and off-road events. The club was only formed a few years ago, but has grown quickly due to the renewed interest in these great fun cars. *Mel Hubbard*

Buggy club events worldwide have continued to grow, with the quality of buggies in attendance becoming even better. The Southern Dune Buggy Club in the United Kindgom regularly attracts 50 or more buggies to its annual gathering and also provides events throughout the year for its members, with everything from cruises to evening social get-togethers.

fee, entry to a club can usually save buggy owners some serious bucks. Many of the street buggies are now so well-finished, heavily chromed, and squeaky clean that their "trailer-trash" image belies the fact they are still perfectly capable of tackling more than the average straight-as-a-die blacktop pavement.

As another example of the more extreme uses of buggies, race builders have realized the potential to turn these flyweight short-wheelbase cars into awesome quarter-milers. Drag-race buggy owners tend to be a more insular group and are more specifically involved with the drag-race community than those with street buggies. Not unnaturally, they are in it for the speed and want to "talk shop" at meetings, races, and the like to keep up with their competitors. Dragsters are such a specialized form of vehicle that—apart from the fiberglass buggy bodyshell—they may have less in

common with the conventional Beetle-based buggy that most clubs cater to. Despite this, it's always great to get information and tips on hotting up your own VW buggy from the experts.

Whichever group you count yourself in, the main thing is to get involved to get the most fun out of buggy ownership. With everything from organized club runs to more serious off-road events, clubs are there to promote buggies and to give owners a good time. Clubs usually set out their booths at the many VW events throughout the year. Over the last few years, buggy clubs have flourished, and their very presence at events has encouraged others to join or even to set up their own club or chapter elsewhere. The Internet revolution has also made it easier for owners to get together online, but there is still nothing to beat the actual personalization of a club than to hold regular events.

Even if you're just looking to buy a buggy or a buggy kit, then clubs are a great place to start. Club members will readily share their experiences—good or bad—of building their particular buggy and give you plenty of ideas for your own. You'll also get to see a wide variety of buggy styles in one place—something that's really useful if you're undecided on which kit to buy. A well-organized club can usually offer discounts on various parts, too—on everything from the actual buggy kits themselves (most manufacturers are part of the club scene) to tires, electrical products, or even insurance. The savings alone will usually cover the cost of any membership charges, plus you get the whole deal with the club facilities and events during the year.

Whatever you want to do with your buggy, the whole scene is a lot more fun when you get involved with others who are like-minded enthusiasts. Even just cruising in a long line of buggies to an event is a great way to make yourself feel special as bystanders can only stand, stare, and feel envious, especially when the sun shines. Right now, the buggy scene—and club membership—is a fast growing part of the whole VW scene, so get your buggy running and get out on the highway!

Many VW owners also own buggies, so why not put them together on a club stand and make them into a prominent display to attract other owners? This cute Manx is a genuine U.S. bodyshell, with the front hood even signed by Bruce Meyers himself. Buggies like these are sure to get others talking to you, so it's no good being shy.

Whatever you drive, you'll have fun on the buggy club scene. This pocket-sized Manx may just be for show, but it's another example of buggy owners' ingenuity. Get out there and start buggin'!

Index

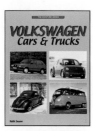

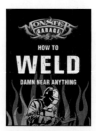